Distributed Denial of Service (DDoS) Attacks

Distributed Denial of Service (DDoS) Attacks

Classification, Attacks, Challenges, and Countermeasures

Brij B. Gupta & Amrita Dahiya

CRC Press
Taylor & Francis Group
Boca Raton London New York

CRC Press is an imprint of the
Taylor & Francis Group, an **informa** business

First edition published 2021
by CRC Press
6000 Broken Sound Parkway NW, Suite 300, Boca Raton, FL 33487-2742

and by CRC Press
2 Park Square, Milton Park, Abingdon, Oxon, OX14 4RN

© 2021 Taylor & Francis Group, LLC
CRC Press is an imprint of Taylor & Francis Group, LLC

ISBN: 9780367619749 (hbk)
ISBN: 9781003107354 (ebk)

Typeset in Times LT Std
by KnowledgeWorks Global Ltd.

To my parents and family for their constant support during the course of this book

— *B. B. Gupta*

To my parents, beloved husband, and my mentor for their motivation throughout the journey of writing this book.

— *Amrita Dahiya*

Contents

Preface

Massive technological breakthroughs have pioneered the complexity, scale, and magnitude of DDoS attacks from a very simple Trinoo platform to the Mirai botnet. The days are gone when DDoS attacks were bound to run iterations for vandalism in the small-scale network. Nowadays, DDoS attacks are a major concern for e-companies, as most businesses rely on online access and the Internet for delivering services, since the Internet was developed for applicability and not security. In addition, enormous development in vulnerable and insecure IoT applications, amplification, and reflective techniques has worsened the situation. Progressively, attackers are always driven by large incentives as compared to the legitimate users or defenders. Consequently, the frequency and intensity of the DDoS attacks is rising at an exponential pace resulting in unparalleled levels of damage. There is no denying the fact that researchers have tried to keep the momentum of proposing defensive mechanisms apace with the massive modernisation of attacking techniques. However, we still lack in a comprehensive and robust DDoS defensive mechanism. Thus, it is very important to analyse the recent trends and different DDoS attack mitigation solutions to explore new research directions.

Distributed Denial of Service (DDoS) Attacks: Classification, Attacks, Challenges, and Countermeasures provides an overview of the basic concepts of DDoS attacks, its different types, modes of attack, and examines the various countermeasures that have been proposed so far. In this book, we discuss the importance of incentives, liabilities, and cyber insurance in any technical solution and have provided a detailed taxonomy of technical and economical defensive solutions against DDoS attacks. Further, the book covers various issues and challenges encountered by different platforms like cloud computing and IoT in dealing with the DDoS attacks. In addition, we discuss SDN and blockchain as the new emerging solutions to DDoS attacks due to their unique and unparalleled features. Features like decoupling of data and control plane in SDN and decentralisation of blockchain can provide promising solutions in this particular domain. The book emphasises the idea of moving from only technical solutions to a proper blend of technical and economical solutions against DDoS attacks. It also outlines the existing challenges and provides an insight into future research directions.

This book is designed for the readers with an interest in the cybersecurity domain, including researchers who are exploring different dimensions associated with the DDoS attacks, developers and security professionals who are focusing on developing defensive schemes and applications for detecting or mitigating DDoS attacks, industrialists who are keen of promoting their security measures or their cyber insurance policies and services with new features, and faculty members across different universities.

The book contains six chapters, with each chapter focusing on bringing an understanding and knowledge of DDoS attacks and their taxonomy along with their defensive mechanisms to the readers. The following list provides a detailed overview of the topics covered in each chapter:

Chapter 1: Fundamentals of DDoS attack: Evolution and Challenges – This chapter introduces the concept of DDoS attacks as a starting point for newcomers to the technology and illuminates some major recent trends and statistics unveiled by well-known organisations across the world showcasing the exponential rise in magnitude, severity, and complexity of DDoS attacks. Further, this chapter discusses the evolution of DDoS attacks and their detailed taxonomy based on various parameters.

Chapter 2: Role of Incentives, Liabilities, and Cyber Insurance – This chapter illuminates the importance of incentives and liabilities in any DDoS defensive mechanism. It highlights cyber insurance and its conceptualisation in the risk assessment process. It discusses the fact that weak defense mechanisms, fragile cryptographic protocols, and loose access control policies are not the only reasons, but the lack of incentives and liabilities also contribute significantly to security breaches.

Chapter 3: Taxonomy of DDoS Defence Mechanisms – This chapter highlights the detailed taxonomy of DDoS defense mechanisms. Apart from this, it also covers open research challenges and issues in any trivial DDoS defense mechanism.

Chapter 4: Taxonomy of Economical Solutions – This chapter discusses the classification of economic defensive mechanisms against DDoS attacks. Various payment schemes, resource allocation schemes, negotiation-based solutions, and Internet pricing schemes are discussed in this chapter. Pros and cons of economic solutions are also discussed.

Chapter 5: DDoS Attacks on Various Platforms – This chapter illustrates DDoS attacks on platforms like cloud computing and IoT. It covers vulnerabilities, issues, and challenges associated with these platforms with regard to DDoS attack. Apart from this, this chapter also highlights taxonomy of DDoS attacks and some significant defensive solutions on cloud computing and IoT.

Chapter 6: Emerging Solutions for DDoS attacks: Based on SDN and Blockchain Technologies – This chapter illustrates some new emerging solutions for handling DDoS attacks, i.e., Software Defined Networking (SDN) and blockchain-based solutions. It also covers advantages of these technologies in mitigating DDoS attacks.

Acknowledgements

Writing a book is not a work of an individual, but it is the outcome of the incessant support of our loved ones. This book is the result of the inestimable hard work, continuous efforts, and assistance of loved ones. Therefore, we would like to express our gratefulness to each one of them who are linked with this book, directly or indirectly, for their cooperation and creative ideas for ameliorating the quality of this book. We would also like to express our appreciation for CRC Press, Taylor & Francis Group, editor and staff for their assistance and unfailing support. We are grateful, from the bottom of our hearts, to our family members for their absolute love and countless prayers. This experience has been both internally challenging and rewarding. Therefore, again, special thanks to all who helped us in making this happen. Finally, we would like to express our gratitude to God by bowing our heads for lavishing on us continuous blessings and the enthusiasm to complete this book.

B. B. Gupta
Amrita Dahiya

About the Authors

B. B. Gupta received PhD in information and cyber security from Indian Institute of Technology, Roorkee, India. He has published more than 250 research papers in International Journals and Conferences of high repute and has visited several countries like Canada, Japan, the USA, the UK, Malaysia, Australia, Thailand, China, Hong Kong, Italy, Spain, etc. to present his research work. His biography was published in the 30th Edition of *Marquis Who's Who in the World*, 2012. Dr. Gupta also received the Young Faculty Research Fellowship award from the Ministry of Electronics and Information Technology, Government of India, in 2018. He is the principal investigator of various R&D projects. He has served as Associate Editor of IEEE Access, IEEE TII, FGCS, IJICS, IJCSE, ACM TOIT, and ASOC, among other journals. At present, Dr. Gupta is working as an Assistant Professor in the Department of Computer Engineering, National Institute of Technology, Kurukshetra, India. His research interests include Information Security, Cyber Security, Mobile Security, Cloud Computing, Web Security, Intrusion Detection, and Phishing.

Amrita Dahiya is currently pursuing her PhD in cyber security under the supervision of Dr. B. B. Gupta at the Department of Computer Engineering, National Institute of Technology (NIT), Kurukshetra, India. She completed M. Tech at Banasthali University, Rajasthan and her dissertation at Jawaharlal Nehru University, Delhi. Amrita received her B. Tech degree from BRCM College of Engineering and Technology, Bahal in 2012. Her research interests include information and cyber security, Web security, denial of service attacks, online social network, and machine learning. She has published several papers in reputed journals and conferences.

Fundamentals of DDoS Attack: Evolution and Challenges

1

Substantial development in technology and digitization is constantly extending the world to new milestones and even more difficult challenges. Cutting-edge technologies like Internet of Things (IoT), cloud computing, blockchain, and many other are capable of pushing, enhancing, and automating the lives of people. However, at the same time, these technologies have added fuel to the fire by appending a long list of vulnerabilities and challenges to the existing perils of Internet. People and businesses have constantly been trapped through attacks and threats by attackers [1]. Further, businesses become more dependent on web connectivity for delivery of services, to carry out critical business operations, and to sustain in the market. All these factors contribute immensely to the daunting growth rate of cyberattacks and threats. A Distributed Denial of Service (DDoS) attack is one of the most common types of cyberattacks and has existed since 1974. It still continues to be a major concern for businesses and security professionals. Therefore, this chapter concentrates on comprehensive details of architecture, variants, evolution, and the challenges of DDoS attacks. Further, this chapter covers recent trends and statistics from reliable sources. It will provide readers deep insights into the security threats corresponding to different variants of DDoS attacks.

1.1 DDoS ATTACK: FUNDAMENTALS

A DDoS attack is a massive, distributed, deliberated, and coordinated attack by multiple compromised machines to overwhelm an online service or a server. Attackers attempt to attack the availability of the service by sending voluminous dummy data to make target machine fall short of resources [2]. There exists a huge misalignment of resources as well as of incentives on the Internet, which provides an easy path for attackers to carry out a DDoS attack. A DDoS attack is a variant of Denial of Service (DoS) attack, where the difference lies in the dispersion of attacking source. In DDoS attack, malicious traffic is generated from multiple distributed sources, while in DoS attack, attack is only from a single source [3]. In this attack, the traffic sent by individual bot machines is not huge enough to disrupt the availability of a service, but it is the result of cumulative effect of efforts made by several bot machines. Attackers usually create a network of compromised machines, i.e., botnet by secretly inserting malicious scripts into them. After taking control of the machines, attackers send spam, distribute malware, and tend to attack other systems by exploiting compromised machine. Apart from this method, attackers tend to exploit vulnerabilities of layers 3, 4, and 5 protocols of Open Systems Interconnection (OSI) reference model, which will be discussed later in this chapter. During early days, this attack was only meant to run a certain set of malicious scripts. But technological advancements and constantly increasing incentives have always placed attackers ahead of defenders. The DDoS attack is a significant risk to online businesses, as few minutes of downtime can have serious repercussions like financial or reputational loss [4]. Now, we will discuss the statistics and recent trends, architecture, and types of DDoS attacks.

1.1.1 Statistics and Recent Trends

The established vulnerabilities and the existing botnets have continuously been explored and exploited by the attackers. The moment a new vulnerability is marked, attackers start working on launching a new series of DDoS attacks by exploiting it. The DDoS attack has always been a preferable choice of attackers, as its mitigation is not as easy as its instigation. The largest DDoS attack, of size 1.7 Tbps, was carried out against Github in 2018 (Figure 1.1) [5]. This attack was considered as the largest attack in history until even more disastrous attack of 2019 joined the race. An unnamed client of Imperva had suffered a DDoS attack with a size of 500 million packets per second. Afterwards,

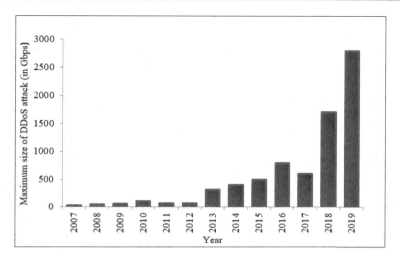

FIGURE 1.1   The largest DDoS attack recorded each year. (Arbour Network Inc.)

the same client had survived an attack with a size of 580 million packets per second in the second quarter of 2019 [6]. Github in 2018 had endured 129.6 million packets per second. Therefore, it can be seen here that in 2019, this attack was almost four times larger than that in 2018.

According to Cisco Visual Networking Index (VNI), by 2022, the number of DDoS attacks will rise up to 14.5 million and may represent 25% of a country's total Internet traffic [7]. Another important trend in this domain is the usage of multi-vector DDoS attack against a single target. In a multi-vector DDoS attack, an attacker tends to merge multiple variants of DDoS attack to not leave any scope for target's survival [8]. Apart from this, another important trend is the usage of "low intensity incursions" that steadily degrade the performance of the target machine over time. These types of attack empower longer attacks that sustain below the threshold value, which can trigger the DDoS defence [44].

In 2019, a company named A10 network had claimed to track approximately 20.3 million DDoS weapons, i.e., infected machines and devices that were available to launch DDoS attack any time [9]. Further, the advent of Internet of Things (IoT) has added fuel to the fire by adding numerous insecure and vulnerable devices to the Internet. These insecure devices are easy to compromise and their abundance has paved a facile path for attackers to create a disastrous botnet. Botnets like Mirai [10], Torii [11], and Daemon bot [12] have proved their fatalness over some past years.

As far as the economic losses are concerned, there is a loss of $12,000 to a small- to medium-sized business due to a single DDoS attack, while it may reach to $2 million for a big enterprise [13]. Next, the COVID-19 pandemic has shaken the world and has bring healthcare and medical services to their knees. However, attackers are continuously leveraging this situation by increasing frequency, complexity, and size of DDoS attack to manifold. This pandemic has made people dependent on remote workforces to meet their requirements. A sharp increase in DDoS attack has been witnessed during the first and the second quarter of 2020 as compared to those of 2019. Apart from this, the average duration has also increased during this period [14]. In February and March, a series of serious DDoS attacks were launched against the US Department of Health and Human services. SYN flooding has been used excessively to perform DDoS attack during this period. Apart from this, Internet control message protocol (ICMP), Transmission control protocol (TCP), User datagram protocol (UDP) and Hypertext-transfer protocol (HTTP) flooding attacks have also been used by attackers to carry out attacks. Most of the attacks are Linux-based, however there is a slight increase in window-based attacks too. Apart from this, ransom-based DDoS attacks are continued to be troublesome for organisations from last few years [15, 16–18].

Nowadays, organisations tend to focus on automation and virtualisation for the availability of their services. However, it is a matter of concern that security evolution could not have compatibility with technological transformation [19]. There is no denying the fact that vulnerable and insecure devices are constantly increasing exponentially, while there is only a mere effort in securing them. Severity and complexity of DDoS attacks can be imagined well through these recent statistics and trends.

1.1.2 DDoS Attack Evolution

The first ever DDoS attack was carried out in the University of Illinois in 1974 [20]. CERL's PLATO terminals had been used to execute command "ext". This command was developed to enable PLATO to communicate with the other external terminals. However, a student, named Davis Dannis, had executed this command on multiple PLATO terminals when there were no external terminals attached to them, which made 31 systems to crash simultaneously. Later, this command was removed to fix this problem. Further, in 1988, a student, named Robert Tappan Morris, developed a code to measure the size of the Internet [21]. However, this piece of code had the capability to replicate itself and it had destroyed almost 60000 nodes over the Internet. This malicious code was named as Morris worm. The next major attack was carried out in 1999 when a macro virus, named Melissa, spread itself through infected file document attached to an email [22]. This virus had the potential to disseminate to 50 more users from the contact list of the user, who opened this infected file. This virus had increased the mail traffic all over the world and forced many big companies to shut down their servers. Further, a major DDoS attack was carried out in the University of Minnesota against an Internet Relay Chat (IRC) server through a public interface [23]. It lasted for two days and 227 zombie machines were used to perform this attack. Trinoo was used for the first time to generate UDP flood [24]. It was the year 2000 that witnessed the most destructive DDoS attack ever. A series of DDoS attacks had been launched to some very big companies like Yahoo, eBay, Amazon, and Dell, which caused the damage of approximately 1.2 billion dollars. Afterwards, attacking Domain Name Servers (DNS) became the new trend in 2001 and 2002. In 2002, all 13 root domain name servers of the Internet had been attacked, which created problem for the legitimate users in navigating the Internet.

The above mentioned events are some of the earlier incidents when the DDoS attack has started to evolve, and has continued to sustain as the most disastrous attack till date [25, 26].

1.1.3 Botnet Structure

Attacking techniques are going through a tremendous transformation from attack performed solely to target infrastructure, to hamper national security, and to create nuisance among people. A large number of compromised machines, i.e., botnets are responsible for these disastrous attacks. First, an attacker looks out for vulnerable and insecure host machines and takes control of them by inserting some malicious script [27]. Afterwards, these compromised machines are instructed to direct their traffic towards a specific target. A botnet usually consists of three components, namely, bot master, Command and Control (C&C) channel, and a large number of bots. Bot master controls these bots through C&C channel. Any protocol, for example, HTTP, TCP and UDP can be used to establish C&C between the bot master and the zombies. Now, we will discuss the different botnet architectures (Table 1.1) [28].

TABLE 1.1 Comparison of different types of botnet structures

FEATURES	ROBUSTNESS	EASE OF IMPLEMENTATION	EFFICIENCY
IRC	Low	Simple	Moderate
P2P	High	Complex	High
HTTP	High	Moderate	High

1.1.3.1 Centralised architecture

In this structure, a central management entity is required to communicate with all bot machines. New instructions are given directly by this entity to the bot agents. This architecture was initially used to perform attacks. Bots are easily detectable through this architecture and, therefore, the attack could also be mitigated effectively. It utilises IRC and HTTP for C&C channel. AgoBot, SpyBot, SDBot, and GTBot are some examples of centralised architecture.

1.1.3.2 Peer to peer (P2P) architecture

Attackers focus on peer to peer architecture to overcome the shortcomings of centralised architecture. Though, in this structure, it is difficult for the bot master to control the army of zombies, it is undetectable and cannot be easily blocked by security mechanisms due to the slow consumption of bandwidth at the same time. In this architecture, a compromised peer acts as the bot master as well as a zombie. It disseminates the malicious instructions to other peers in the same way it receives it from others. PhatBot and Peacomm are the examples of peer to peer kind of botnets.

1.1.3.3 Hybrid architecture

It is very similar to peer to peer architecture. However, the only difference is that bot master establishes peer connection only with the supervisor bots. These supervisor bots have their own separate list of zombie machines, which they don't share with other peers for security purposes. Attack from this botnet is difficult to observe and even more difficult to mitigate. This architecture ensures individualised encryption, symmetric traffic dispersal, less exposure to bots, ease of communication with supervisor bots, and strong connectivity among different botnet entities.

1.1.3.4 HTTP2P (HTTP peer to peer) architecture

Peer to peer architecture was designed to overcome the drawbacks of centralised architecture. However, there exists one disadvantage with P2P architecture, i.e., it is prone to sybil attacks. Therefore, attackers have combined HTTP and P2P to make it more robust. In this structure, supervisor bot encrypts the message and looks out for suitable zombie to deliver the message.

1.2 TAXONOMY OF DDoS ATTACKS

A DDoS attack not only has the potential to make target run out of resources but also has the capability to exhaust them on the intermediate networking path. A DDoS attack has a vast taxonomy as it has many variants [29]. We will discuss taxonomy of DDoS attack in this section according to different parameters.

1.2.1 Types of DDoS Attacks

In this category, we have three types of DDoS attacks, namely, voluminous or flooding attack, protocol-based attack, and application layer attack (Table 1.2). Following are its types:

1.2.1.1 Voluminous attack

In this attack, dummy data requests are generated in ample amount from multiple distributed sources and directed towards a specific node. The main motive of an attacker is to deplete the bandwidth of the targeted node. The attacker takes advantage of the fact that the Internet structure is meant for functionality and not for providing security to the users. Further, amplification techniques aid attacker to scale up the size of the attack. Figure 1.4 shows the HTTP flood attack. For example, in reflective DDoS attack, attacker demands usually a large response from the server in return of small service request [30]. This service request would make server to search all its log files and web pages to generate a proper response, which require enormous resources. Smurf attack and UDP storm attack are some of its examples.

1.2.1.2 Protocol-based attack

In the OSI reference model, every layer has a stack of protocols and every protocol exhibits some vulnerabilities and loopholes. In protocol-based attack, the attackers take advantage of these vulnerabilities to perform a DDoS attack [30, 31]. They tend to exploit mainly layers 3 and 4 protocols to exhaust the processing capabilities and memory of the target node. For example, TCP SYN and ping of death attack.

TABLE 1.2 DDoS attack types

ATTACK TYPE	ATTACK NAME	DESCRIPTION
Voluminous attack	Smurf attack [32]	• ICMP protocol is utilised by network administrators to exchange information about network management and used to check operational status of another device. • An attacker creates a data packet having ICMP message with a spoofed IP address of the victim and then broadcasts it in the network. • Whosoever receives this data packet, will respond to embedded IP packet with a reply which makes victim node flood with ICMP responses.
	UDP storm attack [32]	• Unlike TCP, UDP does not require three-way handshake process to establish connection with the user. • UDP has relatively less overhead in the network and thus effectively used by attackers to perform a UDP flood attack. • "Best effort" data traffic is pushed by attackers through UDP path to overwhelm an online service or machine. • Further, UDP has not any policy for data monitoring or checking, hence this attack is carried out with so much ease and with mere resources.
	DNS amplification attack [33]	• DNS requests are sent with spoofed IP address to DNS server and this would make DNS server to direct all its responses to the target node. • An attacker tends to convert a smaller request into a much larger payload.
	Peer to peer attack [32]	• P2P technology is being widely used for file sharing and downloading and distributed computing. • Unlike conventional botnet, in P2P botnet, an attacker does not communicate with every zombie. • Automated feature of P2P botnet helps in amplifying the attack to a great extent.

Category	Attack	Description
Protocol-based attacks	TCP SYN attack [34]	• An attacker sends a connection request to server using SYN flag to which server responds with an acknowledgement using SYN-ACK flag. • A legitimate client would respond to this SYN-ACK packet with an ACK flag. However, a malicious user exploits this feature and does not send this acknowledgement to the server. • Likely, this would end up in exhaustion of memory at server side as there are a large number of half open connections at server. Server tends to wait for ACK until the timer expires.
	Ping of Death (PoD) [35]	• It exploits basic TCP/IP structure of Internet. • Oversized malformed data packets are sent to the victim using ping command. Generally, maximum payload size of a data packet is 84 bytes. It is not allowed to send a data packet larger than this size. Therefore, an attacker breaks a large-sized data packet into fragments and send them to the victim node. • When victim node reassembles all the fragments, the resultant size is larger than 84 bytes resulting into crashing of server or machine.
	Tear drop attack [36]	• Reassembly algorithm and fragment offset field of IP packet are exploited in this attack. • An attacker creates inconsistency in the fragment offset field of a packet and when all the fragments are reassembled at the server, then overlapping of packets occurs resulting into crashing of server.
Application layer attack	HTTP flood [37]	• A well-planned HTTP flood attack does not require techniques like IP spoofing, amplification methods or tampering techniques. This attack is complete in itself to make a server completely paralyse. • Generally, a user utilises HTTP GET and POST command to communicate with the server. GET is used for retaining static content and POST is used for retaining dynamic content on the web. HTTP POST command usually consumes a large number of resources and an attacker takes advantage of this fact. • It is slow rate attack, and therefore, is difficult to detect.
	Slowloris attack [37]	• Similar to HTTP flood attack, it is also a slow rate attack and sends incomplete information to the server. It makes server to wait indefinitely for the complete information. In other words, an attacker sends HTTP GET request without termination code. • It slowly exhausts the connection capability of server.

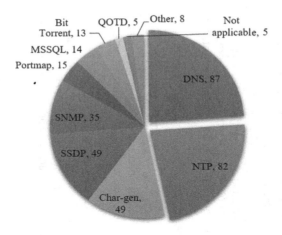

FIGURE 1.2   Targets of application layer attack. (Arbour Network Inc.)

1.2.1.3 Application layer attack

This attack targets the seventh layer of the OSI reference model by obfuscating the web applications (Figure 1.2). This attack is relatively more destructive than the other two types of attacks as it has the capability to ingest network and server resources at the same time. Application layer attacks are the most persistent attacks nowadays. Figure 1.3 shows the different types of protocols exploited by attackers to perform flooding DDoS attack. Figure 1.4 shows the working of HTTP flood attack.

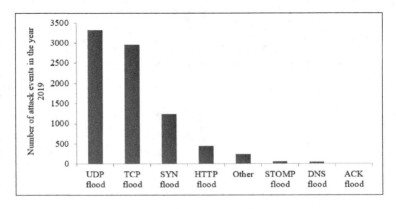

FIGURE 1.3   Types of protocols exploited for flooding DDoS attack.

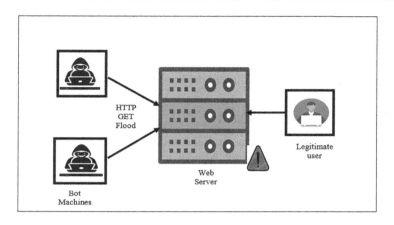

FIGURE 1.4   HTTP flood attack.

1.2.2 Classification Based on Degree of Automation

DDoS attacks can be classified into three categories based on the degree of automation, namely, manual, semiautomatic, and automatic [3], which are discussed below:

1.2.2.1 Manual attack

All phases of the DDoS attack are performed manually in this attack. This method was used during early days, but nowadays, it has become obsolete.

1.2.2.2 Semiautomatic attack

In this type of attack, agent-handler and master-slave botnet architectures are used. An attacker tends to find out the vulnerable systems using automated scanning scripts, and then, malicious codes are inserted into these systems. Further, the attacker instructs these bots to target a specific node through handlers or masters. This attack further falls into categories, namely, direct and indirect attack based on the type of connection between the handlers. In direct semiautomatic attack, an attacker has to embed the IP address of the machine into the malicious code to transform it into a bot. At the moment of attack, in response to the malicious code, the agent has to mark its presence to the handler by showing its availability. The handler has to keep the list of all agents attached to it, which is a major shortcoming of this structure as revelation of one bot can expose all botnets. In indirect semiautomatic attack, an attacker has to rely on some reliable communication protocols between the handlers to avoid the detectability of the botnet for longer duration.

1.2.2.3 Automatic attack

In automatic attack, unlike manual and semiautomatic attacks, all phases of DDoS attack are carried out without any intervention of an attacker. Malicious code programmed with relevant information regarding attack is used to infect the machines.

1.2.3 Classification Based on Vulnerability Exploited

Weaknesses of the system, protocol, and network have always been exploited by the attackers to perform different variants of DDoS attacks. Following is the classification:

1.2.3.1 Volumetric attack

A large number of dummy data requests are forwarded towards the victim to deplete its bandwidth. Please refer section 1.2.1 for detailed information of this attack.

1.2.3.2 Amplification attack

In this attack, the broadcasting feature of an IP network is exploited to scale up size and frequency of a DDoS attack. An attacker tries to generate a small service request, but ensures that the response must have a larger payload size resulting in the exhaustion of resources at server side. DNS amplification and Smurf attacks are the examples of amplification attack, which have already been discussed.

1.2.3.3 Deformed packet attack

In this attack, the IP header of the data packet is falsified or tampered and, then, forwarded to the victim node. Tear drop and ping of death are the examples of deformed packet attack.

1.2.3.4 Protocol-based attack

In this attack, vulnerabilities of layers 3 and 4 are exploited to target processing capability and memory of the target node. Please refer section 1.2.1.2 for detailed information.

1.2.4 Classification Based on Attack Rate

The DDoS attacks can be classified into following three categories based on the attack rate:

1.2.4.1 High rate attack

In this attack, the attacker aims to make online service completely unavailable for longer duration for legitimate users. It is the most destructive than other two attacks.

1.2.4.2 Variable rate attack

In this attack, the attacker varies his rate of sending malicious traffic according to the response generated by the victim machine.

1.2.4.3 Low rate attack

This attack aims to slowly degrade the Quality of Service (QoS) of an online service for legitimate users. This attack sustains for longer duration as it is difficult to detect.

1.3 ATTACK TOOLS

There exist many freely available DDoS attacking tools online. An attacker with naïve knowledge and slight modifications can carry out a DDoS attack with the help of these tools. Table 1.3 lists some of the important attacking tools.

TABLE 1.3   DDoS attack tools

ATTACK TOOL	DESCRIPTION	ATTACK
Mstream [38]	• Counterfeit TCP packets are utilised with ACK flag to perform an attack. • Bandwidth exhaustion attack tool. • Master/slave architecture is employed. • It sends spoofed TCP SYN packet to different servers and broadcasting networks. These servers and broadcasting networks send ACK packets directed towards victim network in response to TCP SYN packets.	TCP ACK
Trinoo [39]	• Bandwidth debilitation tool. • Master-slave botnet is employed to carry out attack against multiple hosts. • IP spoofing is not used by this tool.	UDPfFlooding
HOIC [40]	• Improved version of LOIC. • It can attack 256 targets simultaneously. • Generates ample amount of HTTP GET and POST requests towards application server. • Manual intervention is required for coordination among attackers. • Attacker can easily be traced back.	HTTP flooding attack
XOIC [41]	• More destructive than LOIC. • IP address, port number, or type of protocol need to be specified by the attacker. • Easy tool for naïve users. • Attacker can easily be traced back.	HTTP, UDP, TCP and ICMP flooding attack.
LOIC [42]	• It can perform URL and IP address-based attack. • Attacker's IP address cannot be hidden. • IRC help other users to join in middle of the attack.	HTTP, TCP, UDP flooding attack

Tribe Flood Network [39]	• There is no encryption between handler and attacker or agent and handler. • Command line argument is used to instruct handlers. • It can deplete bandwidth and other resources at target.	TCP SYN, UDP flooding, ICMP. Smurf attack
PyLoris	• Testing tool for servers. • SOCKS proxies and SSL connections are utilised to perform DoS attack. • Various protocols like FTP, SMTP, HTTP, Telnet, and IMPAP can be attacked easily. • Written in Python. • Open TCP connections for as much long as possible.	PyLoris
HULK	• Obfuscated traffic is generated to bypass a caching engine. • Attack detection can be avoided. • Different fields of a web request can be forged easily. • Traffic from HULK can be blocked.	HTTP flooding attack.
Stacheldraht [39]	• Features of Tribe Flood Network and Trinoo are combined with encryption as the added feature. • Uses agent handler architecture. ICMP is used for communication between agent and handler, while TCP is used for communication between client and handler.	ICMP and UDP flooding attack, Smurf attack, TCP SYN attack.
Knight [43]	• IRC-based, a strong attacking tool. • A Trojan Horse program, named back Orifice, is used to compromise a system. • It has a checksum generator.	TCP and UDP Flooding attack. TCP SYN attack.
DDoSim	• All compromised systems create full TCP connection with the victim server. • It generates legitimate HTTP requests to flood the victim.	HTTP and TCP flooding attack.

1.4 CHAPTER SUMMARY

Every business domain has some form of dependency, i.e., direct or indirect on the Internet. This dependency has exposed businesses to various types of cyberattacks and threats. A DDoS attack is one of the cyberattacks, which involves direct implication of Internet structure and uneven distribution of resources over it. This attack is considered as the most generic attack in the sense that it can be carried out at any point in the network. This attack is not peculiar about certain networking requirements. Therefore, it is still continued to be a matter of concern for the whole research community. Hence, the focus of this chapter is to elaborate the DDoS attack, its history, evolution, botnet architecture, and taxonomy. Further, this chapter also contains recent statistics and trends unveiled by some security organisations. Moreover, this chapter also illuminates different variants of DDoS attacks along with widely used attacking tools.

REFERENCES

1. E. Fenil and P. Mohan Kumar, "Survey on DDoS defense mechanisms," *Concurr. Comput. Pract. Exp.*, vol. 32, no. 4, p. e5114, 2020.
2. M. H. Bhuyan, D. K. Bhattacharyya, and J. K. Kalita, "Network anomaly detection: methods, systems and tools," *IEEE Commun. Surv. Tutorials*, vol. 16, no. 1, pp. 303–336, 2013.
3. S. T. Zargar, J. Joshi, and D. Tipper, "A survey of defense mechanisms against distributed denial of service (DDoS) flooding attacks," *IEEE Commun. Surv. Tutorials*, vol. 15, no. 4, pp. 2046–2069, 2013.
4. D. Chaudhary, K. Bhushan, and B. B. Gupta, "Survey on DDoS attacks and defense mechanisms in cloud and fog computing," *International Journal of E-Services and Mobile Applications (IJESMA)*, vol. 10, no. 3, pp. 61–83, 2018.
5. Skottler, "February 28th DDoS Incident Report." 2018.
6. Tomer Shani, "Updated: This DDoS Attack Unleashed the Most Packets Per Second Ever. Here's Why That's Important," 2019.
7. Cisco Visual Networking Index (VNI), "Cisco Predicts More IP Traffic in the Next Five Years Than in the History of the Internet", November 27, 2018. Link available: https://newsroom.cisco.com/press-releasecontent?type=webcontent&articleId=1955935.
8. Marek Majkowski, "The rise of multivector DDoS attacks", The CloudFlare Blog. Link available: https://blog.cloudflare.com/the-rise-of-multivector-amplifications/.

9. A10 networks, "A10 Networks DDoS Threat Intelligence Finds IoT Devices a Growing Part of Global DDoS Weapon Arsenal", SAN JOSE, Calif., March 5, 2019. Link available at: https://www.a10networks.com/news/press-releases/a10-networks-ddos-threat-intelligence-finds-iot-devices-growing-part-of-global-ddos-weapon-arsenals/.

10. J. Fruhlinger, "The Mirai botnet explained: How teen scammers and CCTV cameras almost brought down the internet," India, 2018.

11. Neduchal, Jan, Hron, Martin, Kroustek, Jakub, Iliushin, Vladislav, and Shirokova, Anna (2018), Torii botnet - Not Another Mirai Variant.

12. Georg Wicherski, Markus Kötter, Paul Bächer, Thorsten Holz (2005). "Know your enemy: Tracking Botnets". The Honeynet Project & Research Alliance, pp. 1–17.

13. Kobialka Dan, "Kaspersky Lab Study: Average Cost of Enterprise DDoS Attack Totals $2M.", February 25, 2018. Link available at: https://www.msspalert.com/cybersecurity-research/kaspersky-lab-study-average-cost-of-enterprise-ddos-attack-totals-2m/.

14. Radware, "Smart DDoS Protection During the COVID-19 Crisis", August 4, 2020. Link available at: https://blog.radware.com/security/ddos/2020/08/smart-ddos-protection-during-the-covid-19-crisis/.

15. Kaspersky, "KSN Report: Ransomware in 2016–2017," 2017.

16. R. A. Esraa Alomari, Selvakumar Manickam, et al., "Botnet-based distributed denial of service (DDoS) attacks on web servers: Classification and art." *International Journal of Computer Application (IJCA)*, vol. 49, no. 7, pp. 24–32, 2012.

17. K. Bhushan and B. B. Gupta, "Distributed denial of service (DDoS) attack mitigation in software defined network (SDN)-based cloud computing environment." *Journal of Ambient Intelligence and Humanized Computing, Springer*, vol. 10, no. 5, pp. 1985–1997, 2019.

18. Gupta, B. B. (2011). An Introduction to DDoS Attacks and Defense Mechanisms: An Analyst's Handbook. Lap Lambert Academic Pub. Germany.

19. Gupta, B. B., Dahiya, A., Upneja, C., Garg, A., and Choudhary, R. (2020). "A comprehensive survey on DDoS attacks and recent defense mechanisms." In Handbook of Research on Intrusion Detection Systems (pp. 186–218). IGI Global.

20. Radware, "History of DDoS Attacks," 2017.

21. S. Malenkovich, "Morris Worm Turns 25," 2013.

22. Nota Bene, "A Brief History of DDoS Attacks," 2016.

23. Lee Garber, "Denial-of-Service Attacks Rip the Internet," *Computer (Long. Beach. Calif).*, vol. 33, no. 4, pp. 12–17, 2000, doi: 10.1109/MC.2000.839316.

24. D. Dittrich, "The DoS Project's 'trinoo'distributed denial of service attack tool," 1999.

25. Badve, Omkar P., Shingo Yamaguchi, and Zhaolong Gou, et al., "DDoS detection and filtering technique in cloud environment using GARCH model." In 2015 IEEE 4th Global Conference on Consumer Electronics (GCCE), pp. 584–586. IEEE, 2015.

26. Agrawal, P. K., B. B. Gupta, Satbir Jain, and M. K. Pattanshetti. "Estimating strength of a DDoS attack in real time using ANN based scheme." In International Conference on Information Processing, pp. 301–310. Springer, Berlin, Heidelberg, 2011.

27. R. Puri, "Bots and Botnet: An Overview," Technical Report, SANS Institute, 2003.
28. B. Al-Duwairi, and M. Jarrah, "Botnet architectures." *Botnets: Architectures, Countermeasures, and Challenges*, vol.1, 2019.
29. B. B. Gupta, and O. P. Badve, "Taxonomy of DoS and DDoS attacks and desirable defense mechanism in a cloud computing environment." *Neural Computing and Applications*, vol. 28, no. 12, pp. 3655–3682, 2017.
30. K. Sharma, and B. B. Gupta, "Taxonomy of distributed denial of service (DDoS) attacks and defense mechanisms in present era of smartphone devices." *International Journal of E-Services and Mobile Applications (IJESMA)*, vol. 10, no. 2, pp. 58–74, 2018.
31. Patel, S., Patel, D., and Nazir, S. (2020). Cloud-based Autonomic Computing Framework for Securing SCADA Systems. IGI Global.
32. Lau, F. , S. H. Rubin, M. H. Smith, and L. Trajkovic, "Distributed denial of service attacks." In IEEE International Conference on Systems, Man, and Cybernetics, Nashville, TN, vol. 3, p. 2275–2280, IEEE, 2000.
33. Rossow, Christian. (2014). Amplification Hell: Revisiting Network Protocols for DDoS Abuse. NDSS.
34. CERT Advisory CA-1996-21, Carnegie Mellon University, 2014, https://www uxsup.csx.cam.ac.uk/pub/webmirrors/www.cert.org/advisories/CA-1996-21. html.
35. Ping of Death, 2019, Cloudflare blog [Online]. Available from: https://www. cloudflare.com/learning/ddos/ping-of-death-ddos-attack/.
36. CERT Advisory CA-1997-28, Carnegie Mellon University, 2014, https:// resources.sei.cmu.edu/asset_files/whitepaper/1997_019_001_496176.pdf.
37. C. Enrico et al. "Slow DoS attacks: Definition and categorisation." *International Journal Trust Management Computer Communication*, vol. 1, pp. 300–319, 2013.
38. D. Dittrich, G. Weaver, S. Dietrich, and N. Long, "The 'mstream' distributed Denial of Service Attack Tool." Technical Report. University of Washington, Seattle, USA, 2000, https://staff.washington.edu/dittrich/misc/mstream.analysis.txt.
39. D. Dittrich, "The DoS project's "trinoo" distributed denial of service attack tool," 1999, https://staff.washington.edu/dittrich/misc/trinoo.analysis.
40. HOIC, Sourceforge.net, 2019, http://sourceforge.net/projects/hoic/.
41. XOIC, Sourceforge.net, 2019, http://sourceforge.net/projects/xoic/.
42. LOIC, Sourceforge.net, 2019, http://sourceforge.net/projects/loic/.
43. B.B. King, and D. Morda, "CERT Coordination Centre, CERT Advisory CA-2001-20 Continuing Threats to Home Users." Technical Report, Carnegie Mellon Software Engineering Institute, Pittsburgh, PA, 2001, https://seclists. org/cert/2001/14.
44. Conran Matt, "The rise of artificial intelligence DDoS attacks," 2018.

Role of Incentives, Liabilities, and Cyber Insurance

2

There is no denying the fact that huge interconnectivity of devices on the Internet raises many security issues for organisations and online businesses. Weak defence mechanisms, fragile cryptographic protocols, and loose access control policies are not the only reasons, but the lack of economic aspects, i.e., incentives and liabilities in technical solutions is also responsible for security breaches. This lack of economic aspects forces organisations to invest in defence methods in such a way that the marginal cost is almost equal to the marginal benefit. Therefore, this chapter illuminates the importance of incentives and liabilities in any Distributed Denial of Service (DDoS) defensive mechanism. Further, we also highlight cyber insurance and its conceptualisation in risk assessment process.

2.1 ECONOMIC FACTORS FOR CYBERSECURITY

Cybersecurity and Internet management is an inherently strenuous process because of the huge interconnectivity and dependencies of devices, and also, due to lack of micro-economics in any defensive solution [1, 2]. A rational approach for raising incentives for Internet security can be achieved by assessing vulnerabilities, likelihood of their successful exploitation, and the cost of addressing these vulnerabilities. An organization always has an overhead of legitimising its security cost within security investment, which cannot be handled without knowing incentivisation concept. Researchers believe that security failure is caused more often by bad incentives rather than by bad design [3]. It is a matter of fact that economic solutions have always been ignored by researchers in dealing with DDoS attacks [4–6]. The simple reason behind this is *"Generally, parties defending against threats and attacks are not suffering parties while suffering parties are not defending parties."* This is why despite having so many good technical solutions like cooperative caching and cooperative filtering, we cannot implement them in real time [7, 8]. Therefore, the generation of incentives is not the only matter of concern; in fact, the generation of incentives at the right place of the network and by the right party is also important. Incentive is defined as the motivation inducing a certain behaviour or action of a user that leaves positive externality or payoff on other users. Payoff is the final outcome of cost-benefit analysis [9]. Utility functions help in analysing cost-benefit trade-offs and, hence, used to represent the preferences of participating agents. Therefore, this trade-off analysis arranges the order of outcomes for different choices a user has chosen. If the payoff is positive, then the user will end up having an incentive for a particular action. If it is negative, then the user will be penalised, which is a disincentive. Properly formulated incentives will lead to optimal choices for users; otherwise users will have to opt for sub-optimal choices [10]. We consider an example where a gateway shields a network from various cyberattacks. Due to the action of the gateway router, the end user and the content provider have the maximum benefit. In the case of attack, the gateway router is hardly compensated for any loss by the end user or the content provider. In this example, we do not mean that the end user or the content provider should transfer money directly to the gateway router [11]. In fact, we need to set the incentive chain right among different heterogeneous Internet entities.

Every organisation has a pre-defined security budget from which a fixed part is invested in security methods, tools, and other defence mechanisms. The remaining budget is used to hire a third party, which provides cyber insurance as well as coverage of the organisation's losses. This third party-based cyber insurance depends on the size of the organisation. Therefore, some aspects of economic solution are not feasible for small- to medium-sized businesses. Hence, it is necessary to shield the disadvantages of economic and technical solutions while combining their strengths to build a robust DDoS defence mechanism [12, 13].

2.1.1 Misaligned Incentives

Incentives are as important as technical design in any defensive mechanism. Most of the researches have solely been focused on technical aspects, but risk perception and disproportionate incentives have not been given much consideration [14]. Risk perception is a very important field in security domain as it involves risk assessment for evaluating risks and its associated potential damages [15]. A researcher, named Ross Anderson, discussed the importance of incentives through an example of success of ATMs in the US, while failed in Britain [16]. In Britain, in case of any contention between a user and a bank, the whole liability lies on the user to prove the bank wrong. On the contrary, in the US, the whole liability is on the bank to prove the user wrong in case of any discourse between the user and the bank. Therefore, with the passage of time, people have started losing faith in ATMs in Britain and stopped using them. In the US, this liability on the bank provides incentives to it to deploy security cameras and to invest in information security practices so that no user can cheat them. This is how incentives and liabilities work in case of Internet security too. In this case, banks are in a better position to secure people's money and data; so, there is no harm in assigning more liability to them.

Misaligned incentives have always been leveraged by attackers more efficiently than by defenders. The criminal hacker ecosystem encourages innovation, quick adaptation and effectively directs capital to the lowest cost and the most productive criminal and illicit activities [17]. The main features of criminal economy are decentralisation, support of commoditisation, and competitiveness. On the contrary, in a defensive market, corporate hierarchy slows down the process of decision-making and is non-competitive. According to a survey of 800 IT companies, there exist mainly three incentive mismatches [18]. Table 2.1 lists the main incentive mismatches.

The top elite layer of a hidden economy tends to take advantage of vulnerabilities before they are exposed and patched. One analysis showed that 42% of the revealed vulnerabilities are exploited by attackers within 30 days of release, which implies that if such vulnerabilities were unveiled publicly, the criminal economy would rapidly transform them into new attacks [19]. The black hat economy has a large talent pool and explores freelancing to generate highly specialised products and services. With very low barrier of entry, anybody with naïve technical knowledge can be a part of the black hat economy. This whole black sector consists of a large number of network experts ranging from providers of infected machines to human resource to capitalise on malware kits and hacked identities. This all helps in extensive growth of various illegal businesses through spam, data theft and manipulation, and extortion.

TABLE 2.1 Incentives mismatch on Internet

INCENTIVE MISMATCH	DESCRIPTION
Hackers vs. defenders	• Defenders incentives are always influenced by top-down hierarchy of an organisation. • Attacker's incentives are always influenced by a competitive and decentralised market structure.
Plan of action vs. execution	• According to a report by McAfee, 90% of organisations have policy, provisions and plans for protection against various cyberattacks. However, most of them failed to execute them and these plans only remain in documentation.
Policy-makers vs. policy-runners	• Policy-makers' goals for cybersecurity defenses differ from those of policy-runners. This will definitely affect the effectiveness of the plan. • Different perception of policy-makers and runners about cyber defence leads to inefficiency in strategy development.

On the contrary, Internet users and the white hat community are reluctant to adapt to the benefits of the black hat community. Companies in the grey market primarily serve governments and major businesses whose main objective is intelligence gathering and monitoring [18].

Figure 2.1 shows the map of white and grey hacker market. The white hacker community discloses vulnerability to the public only through vendors. This community does not try to exploit the newly found vulnerability. A grey hat never works for his personal benefits. Figure 2.2 shows the vulnerability map of the black hat community where providers of compromised machines and attacking tools, social engineering, malware developers, and mule herders contribute to various cyberattacks. Table 2.2 lists some of the attributes that should be adopted from black hat economy.

2.1.2 Asymmetries in Information

The announcement of a data breach in information security serves to educate the whole world of a flaw that could have been overlooked and may help other companies defend themselves so it does not become an industry-wide epidemic. For many governments, the question of non-compliance has become very relevant, in fact upcoming General Data Protection Regulation (GDPR) in Europe makes

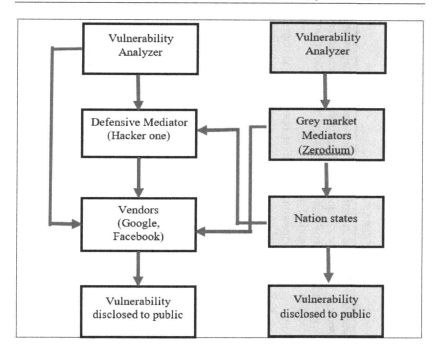

FIGURE 2.1   Vulnerability revelation in the white and grey hat markets.

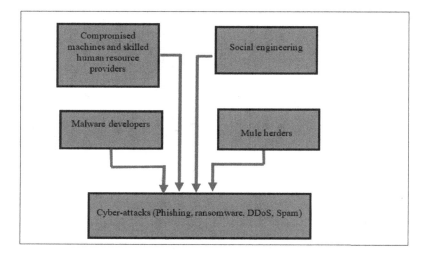

FIGURE 2.2   Vulnerability revelation in the black hat market.

TABLE 2.2 List of features to be adopted from black hat economy

FEATURES TO BE ADOPTED FROM HIDDEN ECONOMY	DEFENDER'S ANALYSIS	ATTACKER'S ANALYSIS
Transparency growth	• Knowledge or information sharing will help minimise the costs to defenders by eliminating redundancy and can help spread awareness about emerging technology and strategies that offer substantial security enhancements.	• Open platforms and advertising campaigns promote the development of innovative new assaults and illegal business models and the rapid acceptance of standard practices.
Incentives alignment	• To equate incentives from leadership to executors, benefits such as promotions and bonuses need to be offered to staff and supervisors that achieve great performance results.	• In the attacker's market, operators at all stages are well-rewarded and punished for under-performance.
Utilize public disclosure	• Responding rapidly to leaks of public vulnerabilities through better patching procedures and faster removal of obsolete systems will increase protection and expense for the attackers.	• Exploiting revealed vulnerabilities prevents costly task of vulnerability search and exploits development, and easily integrates new exposures into attacks to increase benefit until patching is done by defenders.
Lower entry barriers	• Building on a larger pool of expertise, including young people and international information and communications technology (ICT) professionals that are frequently drawn into cybercrime, will help fill the skills void for businesses and drain expertise from the criminal sector.	• The criminal environment, without standardised credentials or territorial restrictions, is able to pull in undervalued expertise from the legitimate economy and optimise its worth.
Market forces	• Substantial utilisation outsourcing and transparent procurement will help cut costs, increase productivity and encourage the widespread adoption of appropriate security technology and tools.	• The transparent and competitive attacker's economy leverages competition and market forces in order to reduce entry barriers and to promote creativity.

it clear that monitoring has to take place very soon after a violation has been detected. Information asymmetries define economic circumstances in which market actors work under conditions of partial details [20]. The problem comes up when one client has more valuable knowledge than another side in a contract. If your company is the victim of a data breach and it is in your knowledge, then interaction with your business partners can cause data breach of their information too. This can affect who you are going to do business with where misuse of their records can adversely impact all other transactions and contracts [21, 22]. Usually, people perceive information asymmetry regarding general transactions or stock purchases. This definition, however, relates to cybersecurity in a very significant way. This is well-acknowledged that real-time information on cyber-crime and data breaches are very minimal. In fact, organisations publishing these data may have an incentive to either over- or under-report: Without reliable reports on cybercrime, it is impossible for companies to generate suitable incentives for better secured software [23]. Lack of data on cybercrime and the harm it causes tend to involve companies and customers have no incentive to invest in cyber defence. There exist three problems that arise from information asymmetry, namely, moral hazard, bad selection, and rationing [24, 25].

2.1.2.1 Adverse selection

Companies that have encountered a serious cyber assault are most keen to buy insurance, resulting in adverse selection. Market insurers attempt to mitigate adverse selection effects through self-selection (e.g., underwriting question-naires), screening (e.g., up-front audits), and signaling (e.g., IT-compliance certificates). In fact, the scarcity of cyber-loss details renders it impossible to categorise businesses into various risk types, thus accentuating the adverse selection problem. This creates dynamics where positive risks get removed from coverage, whereas the negative risks stay in the pool. Signalling problem arises when companies face the challenge of providing cyber-security or privacy poli-cies to users in a trustworthy and sensible way. If such signals are accurate and believable, then they provide the distinction power to users to buy a more secure product from the pool of products. Even if signalling is feasible, it still carries the question, "whether the quality of the signalled product is significant enough to make a considerable proportion of consumers to pay a premium."

2.1.2.2 Moral hazard

Moral hazard problem arises when a user is ready to take higher risks, given he is insured or shielded against the losses incurred due to higher cyber risks. It describes the situation in which a decision-maker doesn't have to endure all costs related to his actions. This issue concerns the likelihood that businesses can lag in their security and monitoring, as it may be more cost-effective for them to just purchase insurance to cover their e-risks. It is the responsibility of an organisation to have acceptable or reasonable level of security. It cannot claim for the losses that incurred due to failure of not having minimal security that every organisation must have.

2.1.3 Vulnerability Trade

"Is public disclosure of vulnerabilities contributing to cyberspace hygienic or not?" Software vendors and security researchers have been discussing this for a very long time. There exists a full-fledged market where trade of vulnerabilities takes place [26]. The demand of vulnerability sales and acquisitions has risen significantly over the last decade. One section of research community believes that availability of source code to all users may prove to be very beneficial as professionals could find vulnerability [27]. On the contrary, other research community tends to believe that if the program code were made accessible to the public, then it would take very little efforts by attackers to detect any new vulnerability.

Anderson [28] in 2002 stated that under certain observations, source code transparency is of equal assistance to attackers and defenders. Another author, Ozment, discussed about immediate disclosure and responsible disclosure [29]. If a vulnerability report is released before its patch is ready, it is called immediate disclosure, while revelation of vulnerability report after patch is designed is termed as responsible disclosure. Immediate disclosure of vulnerabilities would coerce software vendors to immediately provide patches, whereas the users will get encouraged to lessen attack risk. So, we can clearly see that researchers and software vendors have a mixed view on disclosure of vulnerabilities. Software developers ought to realise that the cost of designing secure software is lower than the cost of patching. Beyond expense, vendors suffer reputational risks; how can we overlook the expenses of writing and delivering the patch? A socially mined white hat hacker would submit responsibly to the relevant company in anticipation of a monetary reward if a vulnerability is discovered. In this situation, neither party faces damage because it is now easy for the concerned organisation to fix the vulnerability, hacker earns his reward and there is no cyber threat related to this vulnerability. However, it's an irony that revealing the same risk to black economy is relatively more lucrative. We ought to promote white hat trading as many businesses have launched several projects to provide incentives for disclosing vulnerability. For example, a project name "Project Zero" initiated by Google where full-time analysts are hired to find vulnerabilities and report back to the relevant business [30]. Therefore, investing in addressing vulnerabilities and bugs at the outset of software development should be preferred.

2.1.4 Cyber Insurance

There is an exponential growth in economic costs associated with cyber-crime. Apart from this, the number of organisations that have been adversely affected by cybercrime is also continuously increasing. Cyber risk management is a practice that has been in use for as long as firms have assets to defend [31]. It involves identifying the risks and threats, and applying strategic measures and systematic approaches to ensure that the company is sufficiently secured. Potential cyber risks vary with the type of organisation. Figure 2.3 shows the list of losses covered by cyber insurance. Some companies such as financial sector firms and healthcare institutions have operational issues along with the market issues that need to be handled through a comprehensive risk assessment and management process [32]. Cyber insurance is fundamentally another aspect of risk management for reducing the financial risks of cyber accidents.

Cyber insurance can be a part of a wider risk management plan, which includes detection, assessment, prevention, and tracking of cyber risk exposure [33]. Figure 2.4 shows the vicious cycle of cyber insurance. Cyber insurance offerings often usually provide a wide spectrum of pre- and post-breach services that may lead to lessening the risk ex ante and more effectively mitigating the effects of cyberattacks ex post. Insurance can be treated as just one part of a wider risk control plan for businesses, including an assessment of cyber vulnerabilities for business operations, evaluation of the optimal degree of investment in minimising the danger and determining the residual that may possibly be transmitted to insurance markets [34].

The method of identifying and mapping cyber threats to business operations is not easy. Table 2.3 lists first-, second- and third-party losses covered by cyber insurance. A constantly evolving statutory environment of an organisation generates new exposures and sheer dependence on emerging technologies

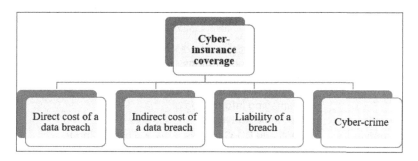

FIGURE 2.3   Losses covered by cyber insurance.

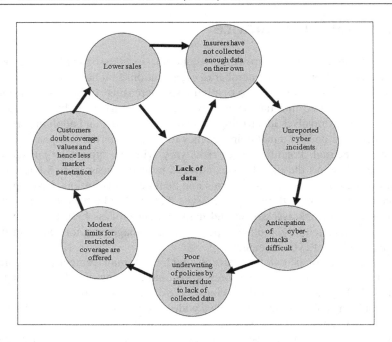

FIGURE 2.4   Cyber insurance cycle.

TABLE 2.3   First- and third-party losses covered by cyber insurance

COVERAGE	CAUSE OF LOSS	COVERAGE FOR THE LOSS
First-party Losses		
Cyber extortion	• Extortion to reveal or pass data or technological assets such as confidential information. • Entrapment to obstruct or interrupt operations. • Extortion for altering, compromising or damaging information or technological assets.	• Costs related to prevent extortion. • Extortion payment cost.
Interruption to business operations	• DoS and DDoS attacks. • Hacking.	• Costs owing to restoration. • Profit loss.

Crisis management	• All combative attacks on data and technology assets.	• Cost for stakeholders feedback and persistent monitoring (for the use of credit cards). • Costs to recover credibility from specialized service provider.
Data security	• Loss or degradation of other intangible properties (e.g., computer software). • A computer attack alters, corrupts or damages critical information assets.	• Cost resulting from replenishment and repairing information. • Cost resulting from replenishment and repairing intellectual property.

Third-party Losses

Network security liability	• Accidental injection of computer viruses causing third-party damage. • Disruption to third party resulting from unauthorised access by insured entities. • Unavailability of resources to users. • Disregarding intellectual rights.	• Costs owing to restoration. • Legal proceedings costs.
Infringement of intellectual rights and the media	• Trademark, software and media reporting breaches.	• Legal liabilities, i.e., cost for defence and claims.
Liability of secrecy	• Dissemination of sensitive data collected or managed by the organisation or within its supervision, possession or control (e.g., attributable to incompetence, malicious actions, damage, and workplace theft).	• Legal liabilities, i.e., cost for defence and claims. • Indirect liability (on outsourcing of information management). • Crisis management (e.g., warning costs to concerned stakeholders, investigations, media affairs, and forensic expenses).

like Internet of Things (IoT), cloud computing, and mobile computing produces new vulnerabilities. Companies need to provide a clear insight of the assets that are vital to their business running and the real-time situations that can impact these assets. The concept of cyber insurance has moral hazard problem. Cyber insurance is a strong component of cyber risk management, but it cannot be viewed as a substitute for the whole cyber risk management process.

Risk assessment is a vital aspect of underwriting cyber insurance policies because cyberattacks have an economic effect on the insurer and any sort of miscalculation or not incorporating a minor element into the formula for determining premiums will leave the business in considerable damage (financial as well as reputational harm) [35]. Risk evaluation approach is faulty from its inception as policy writers believed in considerations such as previous data loss incidents, standards or guidelines established by local regulatory bodies and the IT industry (competitor's regulation structure and business state) [36]. In the past decade, a significant paradigm change has taken place from the conventional risk management approach of just analysing correctly configured and installed firewalls, Intrusion Detection Systems (IDSs) and anti-virus to a modern comprehensive pre-agreement with detailed profile review of the business [37]. Nowadays, risk management activities include not only a standardised overview of company's security profile, but also even more meaningful statistics of the company's state. Figure 2.5 shows the risk management process for cyber-security.

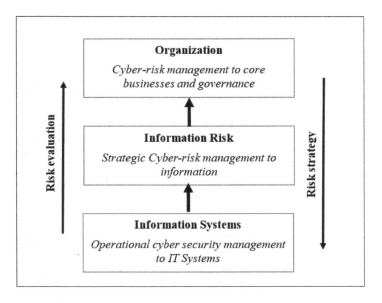

FIGURE 2.5 Cybersecurity risk management process.

Traditional risk management process inadequately identifies ramification of company's security investment in minimising only major risks [38]. But now, businesses in risk management are designing questionnaires or checklists of queries varying from physical protection to cyber vulnerabilities. Checklist has been divided into four categories, namely, organisational, data management, cyber culture or environment, and level of exposure to risks. This new holistic approach of inspecting and splitting the company's profile into different disciplines quantifies the cyber risks differently, efficiently and comprehensively. This new approach checks outsourcing dependencies of the company to check exactly what sort of vulnerabilities or threats, third parties or sub-parties may have introduced to the client's network [39, 40]. In addition to monitoring and evaluating other externalities that might attribute to a data loss event, this approach also checks the cyber culture of an organisation.

2.2 CHAPTER SUMMARY

The emerging technologies continue to impress us, yet advancements in technologies also have implications such as cyberattacks. Researchers have contributed a lot in technological solutions. However, there exists very few research works on economics of cybersecurity. In this chapter, we have tried to highlight the fact that economical solutions are as important as technological solutions. We have discussed economic factors that are barriers in cybersecurity, i.e., cyber insurance (moral hazard, adverse selection), generation of incentives, liability assignment, security and vulnerability trade and risk assessment. Cybersecurity has complex inter-dependencies where action of entity has either positive or negative externality on other users. It cannot be achieved by security measures employed by one organisation. Therefore, it is important for all Internet entities to work with their best features and cooperate with each other in order to compensate for their weaknesses.

REFERENCES

1. Wu, Wu, Y., Fung, R. Y., Feng, G., & Wang, N. (2017). Decisions making in information security outsourcing: Impact of complementary and substitutable firms. *Computers & Industrial Engineering, 110*, 1–12.
2. Kumar, A. (2019). Design of secure image fusion technique using cloud for privacy-preserving and copyright protection. *International Journal of Cloud Applications and Computing (IJCAC), 9*(3), 22–36.

3. Anderson, Ross, & Moore, Tyler. (2006). The economics of information security. *Science, 314*(5799), 610–613.
4. Gupta, Brij B., Ramesh C. Joshi, and Manoj Misra. "An efficient analytical solution to thwart DDoS attacks in public domain." In *Proceedings of the international conference on advances in computing, communication and control*, pp. 503–509. 2009.
5. Agrawal, P. K., Satbir Jain, and M. K. Pattanshetti, et al., (2011). "Estimating strength of a DDoS attack in real time using ANN based scheme." In *International Conference on Information Processing*, pp. 301–310. Springer, Berlin, Heidelberg.
6. Gupta, Brij B. (2012). Predicting number of zombies in DDoS attacks using pace regression model. *Journal of Computing and Information Technology, 20*(1), 33–39.
7. Geng, X., & Whinston, A. B. (2000). Defeating distributed denial of service attacks. *IEEE IT Professional, 2*, 36–41.
8. Naraine, R. (2002). Massive DDoS attack hit DNS root servers.
9. Luong, N. C., Hoang, D. T., Wang, P., Niyato, D., Kim, D. I., & Han, Z. (2016). Data collection and wireless communication in Internet of Things (IoT) using economic analysis and pricing models: A survey. *IEEE Communications Surveys & Tutorials, 18*(4), 2546–2590.
10. Dahiya, A., & Gupta, B. B. (2020). Multi attribute auction based incentivized solution against DDoS attacks. *Computers & Security, 92*, 101763.
11. Gupta, B. B., & Sheng, Q. Z. (Eds.). (2019). *Machine learning for computer and cyber security: Principle, algorithms, and practices*. CRC Press, Boca Raton, FL.
12. Gupta, Brij, Agrawal, Dharma P., &Yamaguchi, Shingo. (Eds.). (2016). *Handbook of research on modern cryptographic solutions for computer and cyber security*. IGI global.
13. Adat, Vipindev, Amrita Dahiya, et al., "Economic incentive based solution against distributed denial of service attacks for IoT customers." In 2018 IEEE International Conference on Consumer Electronics (ICCE), pp. 1–5. IEEE, 2018.
14. Gordon, Lawrence A., & Loeb, Martin P. (2002). The economics of information security investment. *ACM Transactions on Information and System Security (TISSEC), 5*(4), 438–457.
15. Alraja, M. N., Farooque, M. M. J., & Khashab, B. (2019). The effect of security, privacy, familiarity, and trust on users' attitudes toward the use of the IoT-based healthcare: The mediation role of risk perception. *IEEE Access, 7*, 111341–111354.
16. Anderson, Ross. "Why cryptosystems fail." *Proceedings of the 1st ACM Conference on Computer and Communications Security*. ACM, 1993.
17. Kenneally, E. (2019). Economics and incentives driving IoT privacy and security, Pt. 1. *IEEE Internet of Things Magazine, 2*(1), 6–7.
18. Tilting the playing field: How misaligned incentives work against cybersecurity by Mcafee. Link available at: https://www.csis.org/events/tilting-playing-field-how-misaligned-incentives-work-against-cybersecurity.
19. Kathleen Metrick, Jared Semrau, & Shambavi Sadayappan, "Think fast: Time between disclosure, patch release and vulnerability exploitation — Intelligence for vulnerability management, part two," April 30, 2020, Fireeye Blogs.

20. Smith, M. W. (2019). Information asymmetry meets data security: The lemons market for smartphone apps. *Policy Perspectives*, 85–96.
21. Zhang, R., & Zhu, Q. (2019). A game-theoretic cyber insurance framework for incentive-compatible cyber risk management of Internet of Things. *IEEE Transactions on Information Forensics and Security*, *15*, 2026–2041.
22. Wang, J., & Wang, C. (2018). Full secure identity-based encryption scheme over lattices for wireless sensor networks in the standard model. *International Journal of High Performance Computing and Networking*, *12*(2), 111–117.
23. de Bruijn, H., & Janssen, M. (2017). Building cybersecurity awareness: The need for evidence-based framing strategies. *Government Information Quarterly*, *34*(1), 1–7.
24. Woods, D. W., & Moore, T. (2019). Does insurance have a future in governing cybersecurity? *IEEE Security & Privacy*, *18*(1), 21–27.
25. Vagle, J. L. (2020). Cybersecurity and Moral Hazard. *Stan. Tech. L. Rev.*, *23*, 71.
26. Mishra, N. (2020). The Trade: (Cyber) security dilemma and its impact on global cybersecurity governance. *Journal of World Trade*, *54*(4).
27. Xu, Y., D. Tran, Y. Tian, and H. Alemzadeh. "Analysis of cyber-security vulnerabilities of interconnected medical devices." In 2019 IEEE/ACM International Conference on Connected Health: Applications, Systems and Engineering Technologies (CHASE), pp. 23–24. IEEE, 2019, September.
28. Anderson, R. (2002). Security in open versus closed systems—The dance of Boltzmann, Coase and Moore. Technical report, Cambridge University, England.
29. Ozment, Andy. (2005, June 2–3) The Likelihood of Vulnerability Rediscovery and the Social Utility of Vulnerability Hunting, Fourth Workshop on the Economics of Information Security, Cambridge, MA.
30. Versen, M., & Ernst, W. (2020). Row hammer avoidance analysis of DDR3 SDRAM. *Microelectronics Reliability*, 113744.
31. Carfora, M. F., Martinelli, F., Mercaldo, F., & Orlando, A. (2019). Cyber risk management: An actuarial point of view. *Journal of Operational Risk*, *14*(4), 77–103.
32. Russo, P., Caponi, A., Leuti, M., & Bianchi, G. (2019). A web platform for integrated vulnerability assessment and cyber risk management. *Information*, *10*(7), 242.
33. Romanosky, S., Ablon, L., Kuehn, A., & Jones, T. (2019). Content analysis of cyber insurance policies: How do carriers price cyber risk? *Journal of Cybersecurity*, *5*(1), tyz002.
34. Mukhopadhyay, A., Chatterjee, S., Bagchi, K. K., Kirs, P. J., & Shukla, G. K. (2019). Cyber risk assessment and mitigation (CRAM) framework using logit and probit models for cyber insurance. *Information Systems Frontiers*, *21*(5), 997–1018.
35. Khalili, M. M., Liu, M., & Romanosky, S. (2019). Embracing and controlling risk dependency in cyber-insurance policy underwriting. *Journal of Cybersecurity*, *5*(1), tyz010.
36. Liu, M. (2019). *A new paradigm in risk-informed cyber insurance policy design: Meta-policies and risk aggregation*. Regents of the University of Michigan Ann Arbor United States Ann Arbor, MI.

37. Singh, O., & Singh, M. (2020). A Comparative Analysis on Economic Load Dispatch Problem Using Soft Computing Techniques. *International Journal of Software Science and Computational Intelligence (IJSSCI), 12*(2), 50–73.
38. Gavėnaitė-Sirvydienė, J. (2019). Evaluation of Cyber Insurance as a Risk Management Tool Providing Cyber-Security.
39. Nurse, Jason R. C., Axon, Louise, Erola, Arnau, Agrafiotis, Ioannis, Goldsmith, Michael, Creese, Sadie (2020) The Data that Drives Cyber Insurance: A Study into the Underwriting and Claims Processes. In: 2020 International Conference on Cyber Situational Awareness, Data Analytics and Assessment (CyberSA). IEEE (doi:10.1109/CyberSA49311.2020.9139703) (KAR id:80965)
40. Bhattacharya, P., & Guo, M. (2020). An Incentive Compatible Mechanism for Replica Placement in Peer-Assisted Content Distribution. *International Journal of Software Science and Computational Intelligence (IJSSCI), 12*(1), 47–67.

Taxonomy of DDoS Defence Mechanisms

3

The severity, increased frequency, complexity, and intensity of the DDoS attack have resulted in various defensive strategies being proposed. The DDoS attacks can be executed in several ways; thus, one type of approach is not adequate to counter them. With the advances in techniques, tools, and methodologies, novice attackers with trivial resources can circumvent any security system and seem to be a genuine user of the victim machine. Therefore, this chapter illustrates the taxonomy of various DDoS defence mechanisms.

3.1 CHALLENGES IN DDoS DEFENSIVE MECHANISMS

Generally, by the time a DDoS flooding attack is discovered, there is nothing that can be done except to isolate the target from the Internet and resolve the problem manually. The DDoS flooding attacks waste a lot of resources on the pathways that lead to the victim machine; thus, the primary objective of any DDoS protection system is to figure them out as quickly as possible and cease them as close as possible to their origin [1–3]. There exist several challenges in developing a DDoS defensive mechanism that can shield a network from all variants of DDoS attacks. These challenges are discussed below:

- Distributed response: A DDoS defensive mechanism is required that can generate response from multiple scattered points of a network. The most important fact is that the response should be generated cooperatively. Since the Internet is operated in a distributed environment, hence there is no enforcement or guarantee of wide deployment of any defence system or even cooperation between the networks [4].
- Lack of information sharing practice: It is largely believed that media exposure of attacks can cause reputational and brand loss to the company. Due to this fact, organisations do not exercise information sharing practice. Various parameters like attack rate, duration, size of botnet, packet size, type of counter-response generated, its effectiveness, type of damage, etc. are required to design a robust and holistic DDoS defensive mechanism. This could not be achieved without having proper data.
- Lack of large-scale testing: Organisations and researchers lack real-time environment to validate their respective mechanisms owing to the unavailability of large-scale test beds, secure methods of performing live remote trials over the Internet, or comprehensive and real-time-based simulation software that can sustain thousand nodes. Consequently, assumptions about the efficiency of the defensive system are developed based on the small-scale samples and simulations, which are not reliable at all.
- Lack of standardisation and benchmarks: Currently, there is no standard set for attack scenarios or verified, or documented evaluation framework that can allow comparison between the defence systems. This situation would definitely discourage users to invest in the Internet security, as there is a criterion for determining a better product from the large pool of products.
- Economic factors: Parties that do not sustain direct harm from the DDoS attack must deploy a coordinated response system. It suggests an odd economic paradigm, since parties that endure the deployment expenses are not the parties that benefit directly from the scheme. This problem is called tragedy of commons, which can be handled by considering the economic factors. Hence, providing incentives to parties must be the first step towards the wider deployment of a scheme.

Now, we will discuss the detailed taxonomy of DDoS defences. A detailed taxonomy is shown in Figure 3.1.

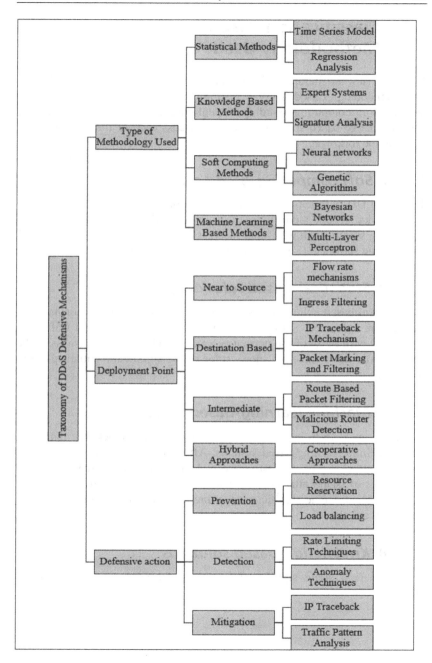

FIGURE 3.1 Taxonomy of DDoS defence mechanisms.

3.1.1 Classification Based on Methodology Used

We will review the literature of different defence approaches based on the various methodologies used. We will distinguish approaches into three groups, namely, soft computing-based, statistical-based, machine learning-based, and knowledge-based solutions. We will discuss each of these solutions in detail in the following sub-sections.

3.1.1.1 Soft computing-based solutions

To combat DDoS threats, soft computation approaches make the use of neural networks, genetic algorithms, Bayesian networks, fuzzy logics, etc. Soft computing systems can withstand inconsistencies and flaws [5, 6]. Table 3.1 shows some significant soft computing-based approaches.

3.1.1.2 Statistical-based solutions

In statistical-based solutions, regular statistical values for the normal traffic flow are computed. Subsequently, statistical values of current traffic are contrasted with those of the normative values to check maliciousness of the actual traffic flow. Table 3.2 shows some of the significant statistical-based solutions.

3.1.1.3 Machine learning-based solutions

There is a need to train the security framework with attack-free data traffic in machine learning-based systems. Afterwards, the trained framework classifies attack traffic as destructive or legitimate. The most widely used approaches to DDoS attacks are machine learning-based solutions [27–30]. Table 3.3 shows some significant machine learning-based solutions against the DDoS attacks.

3.1.1.4 Knowledge-based solutions

Table 3.4 lists some significant knowledge-based solutions for DDoS attacks.

TABLE 3.1 Soft computing-based DDoS defensive mechanisms

AUTHORS	METHODOLOGY USED	LIMITATIONS
Li et al. [7]	Transductive Confidence Machines in K-Nearest Neighbours (TCM-KNN) algorithm is used to discover DDoS attack. In addition, requirements and anomalies of end users having significant effect on the network are processed to develop an effective anomaly detection system.	This mechanism possesses low accuracy and high false positive rate.
Rahul et al. [8]	TCP and SIP flooding attacks are detected using VoIP Flood Detection System. Genetic algorithm has been used for user authentication.	The main drawback of this scheme is that it is vulnerable to flooding attacks. In fact, it is very similar to HTTP, i.e., this protocol can produce a reply to every request, even for the dummy or fake request.
Wei et al. [9]	This scheme aims to figure out how the correlation varies during a DDoS attack. Traffic flow is first analysed using Extended First Connection Density (EFCD) and the cross-correlation function is used for correlation assessment. In addition, fuzzy rules are used for grouping and accuracy assurance.	Only specific types of DDoS attacks are detectable.
Gonzalez et al. [10]	A trust-based model has been developed using Bayesian inference model, which tests the reliability of router w.r.t. transmitting data without falsifying its IP address. System performance with the deployment of this model is analogous with the performance without its deployment.	IP spoofing is difficult to identify because the routers are placed in a dispersive manner.

(Continued)

TABLE 3.1   Soft computing-based DDoS defensive mechanisms (*Continued*)

AUTHORS	METHODOLOGY USED	LIMITATIONS
Shiaeles et al. [11]	Fuzzy estimators are used to calculate the arrival time of the data packets. This system is able to find malicious IPs in real time.	It is unable to detect malicious IPs where data flow is dispersed, i.e., at source itself. It can't mitigate flash crowd-based attacks.
Wang and Yang [12]	Self-adaptive fuzzy rules are used along with variance time plots to discover DDoS attacks.	Operating costs of managing Fuzzy Judger as DDoS attack rules need to be defined along with their Fuzzy values.
Lee et al. [13]	Genetic algorithm is utilised to augment the DDoS detection rate. An updated hash function is used to reduce collision numbers to boost the traffic vector. Additionally, the packet-based window size is used to lessen computational overload.	It cannot identify DDoS attack during flash crowd events.
Vijayasarathy et al. [14]	It is a Naive Bayesian-based DDoS detection mechanism. It is lightweight in nature and works closely to line speeds.	This method was only tested for TCP and UDP-based DDoS attacks.
Haider et. al. [15]	A host anomaly detection system (HADS) based on Fuzzy Rough Set Attribute Reduction (FRAR) and Gaussian Mixture Model (GMM) has been proposed in this paper. It is designed to detect zero-day attacks from Linux systems.	It is competent to identify the attacks that have signatures already in syscall-ids and elapsed time. It is performed only on a specific data set.
Velliangiri and Pandey [16]	A Fuzzy and Taylor-Elephant Herd optimisation (FT-EHO) based on Deep Belief Network (DBN) has been proposed to detect DDoS attack in cloud environment.	There is computational overhead due to multiple hidden layers.

TABLE 3.2 Statistical-based DDoS defensive mechanisms

AUTHORS	METHODOLOGY USED	LIMITATIONS
Cheng et al. [17]	Spectral analysis is utilised to detect DoS attacks. This scheme has higher accuracy due to low false positive rates of attacker identification.	It can handle only TCP-based DoS attacks.
Mirkovic et al. [18]	This scheme aims at defending DDoS attack by scanning and analysing inbound and outbound traffic from source and comparing it with pre-specified nominal traffic profile.	It depletes large memory and processing power.
Zhang et al. [19]	Auto Regressive Integrated Moving Average (ARIMA) model is used along with the previous rounds service rates to discover DDoS attacks.	Low rate DDoS attacks and TCP flows are considered only to validate the proposed model.
Cheng et al. [20]	Four traffic flow features are considered to discover DDoS attacks, namely, traffic flow volume, non-uniformity in the flow, dispersion of source IP addresses, and congregation of destination IP addresses.	Large database of these four values for every traffic flow needs to be maintained.
Peng et al. [21]	Bandwidth DDoS attack is detected using frequency of coming data requests from new IP addresses. Accuracy rate is improved using sequential non-parametric change point detection method.	There are expenses on maintaining a database of old connections. Before targeting the server, attackers might trick it by transmitting seemingly legitimate traffic from the bot machines to get acceptance into the database.
Udhayan and Hamsapriya [22]	A Statistical Segregation Method (SSM) is used to identify DDoS attacks. Under this scheme, data are sampled under sequential time intervals and, then, the sampled data are related to attack state conditions.	There exists inaccuracy when assessing threshold and behavior of data flow traffic. Short length sampled data result into inaccuracy.

(Continued)

TABLE 3.2   Statistical-based DDoS defensive mechanisms (*Continued*)

AUTHORS	METHODOLOGY USED	LIMITATIONS
Oke and Lukas [23]	Prompt actions and statistical characteristics of data are collected and can be used to track DoS attack in the longer term. The goal here is to pick the input attributes that do not cause high computing costs on the server.	No provision is made for detecting DDoS attacks when attackers send traffic from disparate locations.
Chen et al. [24]	Change Aggregation Trees (CAT) are used along with Distributed Change Point (DCP) to discover DDoS attacks.	It can handle only a certain kind of DDoS attack. In addition, it is such a non-parametric DDoS detection method whose function is focused solely on the observed traffic flow features.
Dainotti et al. [25]	Volume-based anomalies are monitored to detect DoS attacks. Continuous wavelet transformation is used along with change point detection method.	This model is not validated on DDoS attacks since it is tested on anomaly free traffic flows.
Kalkan et al. [26]	A joint entropy-based security scheme has been proposed to defend against DDoS attacks in the Software-defined Networking (SDN) environment.	There exist issues of scalability and overhead as data packets passing through switches must be first sent to the controller. Moreover, there is a need of separate nominal profiles for different timings of a day.

TABLE 3.3 Machine learning-based DDoS defensive mechanisms

AUTHORS	METHODOLOGY USED	LIMITATIONS
Zhong and Yue [31]	Features are extracted from normal traffic using Fuzzy C-means (FCM) cluster algorithm and association model to identify DDoS and unknown attacks.	There exist operational costs to maintain database with regular traffic patterns.
Li and Lee [32]	Wavelet analysis dependent energy distribution mechanism is utilised to prevent DDoS attacks.	Parameters like packet IP address distribution and connections which could enhance detection rate are not considered while validating the proposed approach.
Seo et al. [33]	False positive rate is minimised using multiple Support Vector Machines (SVMs). The frequency of a particular type of packet is determined using traffic rate analysis.	It can handle only a certain kind of DDoS attack. There is computational overhead of system training.
Lee et al. [34]	The precursors of DDoS attacks are determined using cluster analysis. This mechanism is simple to implement because normalised distance is explored to form different groups.	It can detect only a certain type of DDoS attacks. It has been validated on single dataset.
Yu et al. [35]	The SVM is used for attack classification, while Simple network management protocol (SNMP) Management information base (MIB) statistical data are utilised to detect DDoS attacks. Moreover, it is lightweight in nature and the attack detection rate is higher.	If the attacker manipulates MIB data then this mechanism is unable to mitigate DDoS attack.
Hwang et al. [36]	Data mining learning process is used secure a public network from getting compromised. This mechanism is named as Netshield.	There exist operational costs of developing security database. This scheme is validated on the locally generated dataset.
Rahmani et al. [37]	Joint entropy analysis is used to detect multiple traffic distributions. It is distributed in nature.	Degree of coherence is calculated based on the observed traffic volume and confirmed connections per unit time. There is a need to consider more variables to make it more robust.

TABLE 3.4 Knowledge-based DDoS defensive mechanisms

AUTHORS	METHODOLOGY	LIMITATIONS
Thomas et al. [38]	It is a localised mechanism for packet filtering, which distinguishes DDoS traffic from flash crowd by inline processing. The mechanism is named as Netbouncer. An important feature of this scheme is that it does not store historical data or generalise any attack signature.	Usage of hash-based message authentication code (HMAC) and cryptography augments overhead on the system.
Limwiwatkul and Rungsawang [39]	TCP/IP packet header information is evaluated and checked with predefined rules or attack signatures for any sort of inconsistency in the data packet.	Analysing every data packet incurs a large overhead on the system.
Wang et al. [40]	An Augmented Attack Tree (AAT) framework is utilised to represent DDoS attacks. Potential threats due to malicious packets in a data flow are assessed using this AAT structure. Next, all variants of DDoS attacks are detected using bottom-up AAT algorithm.	The AAT can model only known variants of DDoS attack. It is not a distributed solution; therefore, it can suffer through single point failure.
Gil and Poletto [41]	A scheme named Multi-Level Tree for Online Packet Statistics is developed, which is a tree data structure. Malicious data packets at the edge of a source network are filtered by routers utilising this structure.	The key downside of this scheme is that it is vulnerable to attack memory depletion, as it uses dynamic tree structure to record packet rate for each local network IP address.
Lu et al. [42]	Feature extraction and DDoS detection have been carried out using temporal and spatial correlation, respectively. 97% accuracy has been achieved using this scheme.	The only downside to this strategy is that data packets from new links would be knocked out during the attack time.
Zhang and Parashar [43]	It is a peer to peer overlay-based approach where each node in the intermediate network exchanges information about the attack with monitoring nodes distributed over the top network.	If the attacker wants to conduct low rate or possibly genuine DDoS attacks, the nodes cannot recognise DDoS attacks.

3.1.2 Taxonomy Based on Deployment Point

In this segment, we will address defence approaches for network/transport level DDoS attacks in the categories, namely, close to source, close to destination, intermediate network routers, and hybrid solutions. We will discuss each category in detail in following sub-sections.

3.1.2.1 Near to source-based solutions

In this section, we address defence mechanisms that are implemented near the origin of the attacks. These defensive processes are centralised in nature. Centralised points to the belief that mechanism-led defensive action only takes place at a basic hub in a network. This kind of solution provides benefits as well as drawbacks against DDoS attacks. The advantage of this kind of solution is that it is the best practice to stop attack at its initial stage and prevent the malicious data traffic from disseminating into the network. However, its disadvantages have more serious implications than its advantage. The sources of attack traffic are scattered (distributed) across the network, and data traffic from a single source is not significant enough for local Internet service provider (ISP) or local security systems to track. Therefore, it is not feasible to deploy defensive mechanism to monitor every node in the network. Most importantly, a question arises, "Who will pay the deployment costs of near to source-based mechanism: insured or insure?" Now, Table 3.5 shows some of the significant near to source-based defence mechanisms.

3.1.2.2 Near to destination-based solutions

Likely, close to source-based defensive mechanisms, these defensive mechanisms cannot properly filter off attack traffic as attack traffic is heavily regulated at the victim network boundaries. Being so in pro-active mode or in filtering, there is always some malicious traffic that reached the target server. Table 3.6 shows some destination-based DDoS defensive mechanisms.

3.1.2.3 Defensive mechanisms deployable at intermediate routers

These structures are typically implemented between the source and the destination at any intermediate routers. These types of solutions overcome the limitations of near to source or destination-based mechanisms. Now, we will discuss the significant intermediate solutions.

TABLE 3.5 Near to source-based DDoS defensive mechanisms.

METHODOLOGY	PAPERS
Filtering at the edge routers:	• These mechanisms usually filter out IP spoofed attack packets at the edge routers of the network. • In [44, 45], IPSec protocol has been proposed to tackle IP spoofing in IPV4 and IPV6 packets. The drawbacks of these solutions are complexity and increased overhead. • In [46], authors suggested a method for detecting infiltrations to counter DoS attacks. Ingress filtering on edge routers essentially reduces the effects of spoofing of IP addresses. • The key drawback of this strategy is that if the spoofed IP address is still within the correct IP address set, then the spoofed IP packet will quickly past the ingress/egress filtering protocols.
D-WARD (DDoS Network Attack Recognition and Defence) [18]	• This scheme is intended to safeguard a network by analysing and evaluating incoming and outgoing traffic from source, and comparing it with the pre-defined normal traffic profile to find any discrepancy. • The main drawback of this scheme is that it consumes a significant amount of memory and processing power. • Identification and refusal of attack traffic is performed at the edge routers.
Flow rate-based mechanisms	• MULTOPS [41] is a tree-based data structure used by the router to track and monitor malicious traffic at the source network edge. • It is based on the assumption that the rate of change of inbound traffic is directly proportion to the outbound traffic. • The main drawback of this scheme is that it is susceptible to memory exhaustion attack as it utilises a dynamic data structure to store values. • Another TOPS method [47] employs hash tables and distribution of probability functions to track packets in a network. It is also based on the same assumption discussed above. • In case of multimedia requests, this assumption leads to completely failed in MULTOPS and TOPS.
Reverse firewall	• Reverse firewall secures the complete Internet from a local network, i.e., tests outgoing traffic from a local network. • A reverse firewall interrupts the transfer rate of packets that no other Internet host calls for. • The downside of this mechanism is that the operation needs manual control.

TABLE 3.6 Near to destination-based DDoS defensive mechanisms

METHODOLOGY	PAPERS
IP traceback mechanisms	• Traceback is the method for discovering the real IP address (source) of malicious attack packets used to execute attacks, rather than locating their spoofed IP address [48]. • Packet marking scheme [49–51] use the traceback concept by tagging every data packet targeted for a network. • Routers in the route between source and victim network identify each data packet with a special specifier that lets victim network map back to its actual source. • These schemes have high false positive rate. • Link testing [52, 53] is another method that the victim network uses to trace illegitimate data packets back.
Management Information Base (MIB) [54]	• An MIB is a database related to data packets and network routing information. It can be easily inferred that network is under DDoS attacks or not by continuously monitoring the MIB details. • This method is effective as it can easily analyse anomaly in ICMP, UDP, and TCP packets by identifying statistical patterns and finding out the type of DDoS attack.
Packet marking and filtering mechanisms	• Packet marking systems tend to mark the legitimate packets with the travel route from source to destination, which allows routers to differentiate malicious data packets from the legitimate ones [55, 56]. • These mechanisms have dynamic filtering provisions by allowing intermediate routers to filter out malicious packets. • Hop count filtering seeks to filter the attack packets based on the hop count. Destination is used to store IP address of the source and its adjacent hops when no attack occurs. • Packet score [57], a score-based packet dropping mechanism has been proposed in which data packet legitimacy is checked utilising scores of the given input variables. It is inefficient towards low rate DDoS speeds. • Probabilistic filter scheduling is a collaborative filtering method in which filter is perpetrated to an optimal position closer to attack.

- Malicious routers detection and filtration: Attackers can also use intermediate routers for DDoS attack amplification. There exist several ways to prevent intermediate routers from being hacked [58]. In [59], the system, named watchers, detects routers which diverge from regular behavior, i.e., by discarding or misrouting packets. A legitimate router may be misidentified as an illegitimate one if the attackers deliver spoofed packets. Intermediate routers need high computing capacity to identify and counter DDoS attacks, but repetitive detection and response by every router on the path wastes valuable resource.
- Route-based packet filtering: Like ingress filtering which functions at edge routers, it uses the same concept at core routers. It requires information about the network structure for proper functioning [60]. This system operates on the idea that every core router has a limited set of source IP addresses. Any data packet having spoofed IP address cannot escape via intermediate routers. A big limitation to this method is that if the attacker uses non-IP spoofed packets to execute the attacks, then this method cannot strip out malicious packets.

3.1.2.4 Hybrid solutions

Defensive measures against DDoS attack implemented either at the source or at the destination or on the intermediate router have no coordination from the other Internet entities. They operate in a secluded way without any cooperation from the rest of the Internet, which is the biggest limitation of all of the defensive solutions discussed above. Hybrid solutions have distributed structures where different modules coordinate with each other to fight against any cyberattack. Distributed defensive solutions are deployed across the Internet at different locations, and each entity functions according to its ability and cooperates with the other entities. Table 3.7 lists some significant cooperative solutions.

3.2 CHAPTER SUMMARY

In this chapter, we have discussed the seriousness and severity of DDoS attacks on the global economy. Apart from that, a comprehensive classification of DDoS attacks has been discussed. Further, a holistic classification

TABLE 3.7 Cooperative solutions for DDoS attacks

METHODOLOGY	PAPERS
Signature-based cooperative defence mechanism [62, 63]	• COSSACK [61] uses a software program named Watchdog, which consists of all edge network's border routers. It is based on the attack signatures, the ability of the edge router to filter out malicious attacks by using attack signatures and the uninterrupted connection between the Watchdogs. • This solution has the disadvantage that it cannot mitigate DDoS attacks in legacy networks that do not use the COSSACK mechanism.
Packet marking and filtering-based cooperative solutions [64]	• Decentralised packet marking and filtering mechanisms tend to detect attack. • In [65], a cooperative pushback mechanism has been proposed against multi-traffic flow aggregate. An aggregate may be a sub-set of packet flows with similar characteristics, i.e., specific source IP addresses or packets intended for a particular port, or packets containing HTTP-based or TCP SYN-based or ICMP ECHO-based requests. • In [66], the pushback function has been used to alert upstream routers to rate limit the traffic. However, if the attack is uniformly spread, certain approaches would not be successful. • In [67], a cooperative approach called Attack Diagnosis (AD) has been proposed, which combines packet marking and pushback schemes to alleviate DDoS attacks. One drawback of this mechanism is that it isn't intended for large-scale attacks. • Parallel attack diagnosis (PAD), an extension of AD, will concurrently detect and filter the traffic attacks from several routers. It is successful against large-scale DDoS attacks.
Datagram-based cooperative solution	• In [68], a filter-based system called Active Internet Traffic Filtering (AITF) has been developed where recipient is permitted to contact attacking sources and alert them to stop delivering malicious requests. • Local ISPs must have some sort of incentives to be a part of this mechanism, i.e., either local ISP should provide aid to AITF for monitoring its malicious nodes or AITF should disconnect its access to the server. • Major drawback to this scheme is that when traffic originates from outside the network of AITF, then attack traffic could not be handled by server.

(Continued)

TABLE 3.7 Cooperative solutions for DDoS attacks (*Continued*)

METHODOLOGY	PAPERS
Capability-based cooperative defence solutions	• Senders must procure short-term permissions from the receiver in capability-based systems in order to send packets to the receiver. This will act as a token, which is to be appended to every data request sent by the users. • Distributed testing centres in the network test the packets' legitimacy before forwarding to the next node and prioritise these tokenised packets at the time of the attack. For example, see [69, 70]. • High processing costs and memory overhead are drawbacks in capability-based programs.
Anomaly-based cooperative solution [71]	• In [72], a hybrid collaborative defensive mechanism, named Stoplt, has been developed, where every receiver in a network is permitted to deploy a network filter that prevents the infiltration of the malicious traffic. • Source nodes are authenticated using Passport [73]. • It can provide uninterrupted transmission during a broad range of DDoS attacks.
DEFensive Cooperative Overlay Mesh (DEFCOM)	• DEFCOM [74] is a distributed defence mechanism that integrates heterogeneous nodes and lets them share information to effectively defend against DDoS attacks. It is an overlay solution where the existing infrastructure facilitates in its deployment. • Every node is intended to act any of these entities, namely, alert generator, rate limiter, and distinguishing nodes.
SPIFFY [75]	• In this mechanism, a short-term contract is generated between the bottleneck of a network and the traffic sources. • It is based on the assumption that the legitimate users do not tend to increase their data sending rate, but malicious users do the same.

of defensive solutions has been presented along with their advantages and disadvantages. We have also discussed the importance of a solution, which is distributed, widely deployable, cooperative, and incentive provider to the users and local ISPs.

REFERENCES

1. K. Bhushan and B. B. Gupta, "Security challenges in cloud computing: state-of-art," *International Journal of Big Data Intelligence*, vol. 4, no. 2, pp. 81–107, 2017.
2. P. Sharma, J. Sengupta, and P. K. Suri, "Survey of intrusion detection techniques and architectures in cloud computing," *International Journal of High Performance Computing and Networking*, vol. 13, no. 2, pp. 184–198, 2019.
3. B. B. Gupta, S. Gupta, and P. Chaudhary, "Enhancing the browser-side context-aware sanitization of suspicious HTML5 code for halting the DOM-based XSS vulnerabilities in cloud," *International Journal of Cloud Applications and Computing (IJCAC)*, vol. 7, no. 1, pp. 1–31, 2017.
4. J. K. Chahal, A. Bhandari, and S. Behal, "Distributed denial of service attacks: A threat or challenge," *New Review of Information Networking*, vol. 24, no. 1, pp. 31–103, 2019.
5. B. B. Gupta, D. P. Agrawal, S. Yamaguchi, and M. Sheng, "Advances in applying soft computing techniques for big data and cloud computing," 2018.
6. O. Singh and M. Singh, "A comparative analysis on economic load dispatch problem using soft computing techniques," *International Journal of Software Science and Computational Intelligence (IJSSCI)*, vol. 12, no. 2, pp. 50–73, 2020.
7. Y. Li, L. Guo, Z.-H. Tian, and T.-B. Lu, "A lightweight web server anomaly detection method based on transductive scheme and genetic algorithms," *Comput. Commun.*, vol. 31, no. 17, pp. 4018–4025, 2008.
8. A. Rahul, S. K. Prashanth, B. Suresh Kumar, and G. Arun, "Detection of intruders and flooding in VoIP using IDS, Jacobson fast and Hellinger distance algorithms," *IOSR J. Comput. Eng.*, vol. 2, no. 2, pp. 30–36, 2012.
9. W. Wei, Y. Dong, D. Lu, and G. Jin, "Combining cross-correlation and fuzzy classification to detect distributed denial-of-service attacks," in International Conference on Computational Science, 2006, pp. 57–64.
10. J. M. Gonzalez, M. Anwar, and J. B. D. Joshi, "A trust-based approach against IP-spoofing attacks," in 2011 Ninth Annual International Conference on Privacy, Security and Trust, 2011, pp. 63–70.
11. S. N. Shiaeles, V. Katos, A. S. Karakos, and B. K. Papadopoulos, "Real time DDoS detection using fuzzy estimators," *Comput. Secur.*, vol. 31, no. 6, pp. 782–790, 2012.
12. J. Wang and G. Yang, "An intelligent method for real-time detection of DDoS attack based on fuzzy logic," *J. Electron.*, vol. 25, no. 4, pp. 511–518, 2008.

13. S. M. Lee, D. S. Kim, J. H. Lee, and J. S. Park, "Detection of DDoS attacks using optimized traffic matrix," *Comput. Math. with Appl.*, vol. 63, no. 2, pp. 501–510, 2012.
14. R. Vijayasarathy, S. V. Raghavan, and B. Ravindran, "A system approach to network modeling for DDoS detection using a Naive Bayesian classifier," in 2011 Third International Conference on Communication Systems and Networks (COMSNETS 2011), 2011, pp. 1–10.
15. W. Haider, N. Moustafa, M. Keshk, A. Fernandez, K. K. R. Choo, and A. Wahab, "FGMC-HADS: Fuzzy Gaussian mixture-based correntropy models for detecting zero-day attacks from Linux systems," *Computers & Security*, 101906, 2020.
16. S. Velliangiri and H. M. Pandey, "Fuzzy-Taylor-elephant herd optimization inspired deep belief network for DDoS attack detection and comparison with state-of-the-arts algorithms," *Future Generation Computer Systems*, vol. 110, pp. 80–90, 2020.
17. C.-M. Cheng, H. T. Kung, and K.-S. Tan, "Use of spectral analysis in defense against DoS attacks," in Global Telecommunications Conference, 2002. GLOBECOM'02, *IEEE,* 2002, vol. 3, pp. 2143–2148.
18. J. Mirkovic, G. Prier, and P. Reiher, "Attacking DDoS at the source," in 10th IEEE International Conference on Network Protocols, 2002, Proceedings, 2002, pp. 312–321.
19. G. Zhang, S. Jiang, G. Wei, and Q. Guan, "A prediction-based detection algorithm against distributed denial-of-service attacks," in Proceedings of the 2009 international conference on wireless communications and mobile computing: Connecting the World wirelessly, 2009, pp. 106–110.
20. J. Cheng, J. Yin, C. Wu, B. Zhang, and Y. Liu, "DDoS attack detection method based on linear prediction model," in International Conference on Intelligent Computing, 2009, pp. 1004–1013.
21. T. Peng, C. Leckie, and K. Ramamohanarao, "Proactively detecting distributed denial of service attacks using source IP address monitoring," in International conference on research in networking, 2004, pp. 771–782.
22. J. Udhayan and T. Hamsapriya, "Statistical segregation method to minimize the false detections during DDoS attacks," *IJ Netw. Secur.*, vol. 13, no. 3, pp. 152–160, 2011.
23. G. Öke and G. Loukas, "A denial of service detector based on maximum likelihood detection and the random neural network," *Comput. J.*, vol. 50, no. 6, pp. 717–727, 2007
24. Y. Chen, K. Hwang, and W.-S. Ku, "Distributed change-point detection of DDoS attacks over multiple network domains," in Int. Symp. on Collaborative Technologies and Systems, 2006, pp. 543–550.
25. A. Dainotti, A. Pescapé, and G. Ventre, "A cascade architecture for DoS attacks detection based on the wavelet transform," *J. Comput. Secur.*, vol. 17, no. 6, pp. 945–968, 2009
26. K. Kalkan, L. Altay, G. Gür, and F. Alagöz, 2018 "JESS: Joint entropy-based DDoS defense scheme in SDN," *IEEE Journal on Selected Areas in Communications*, vol. 36, no. 10, pp. 2358–2372.
27. Gupta, B. B. (Ed.). (2018). Computer and Cyber Security: Principles, Algorithm, Applications, and Perspectives. CRC Press.

28. Gupta, B. B., Perez, G. M., Agrawal, D. P., & Gupta, D. (2020). Handbook of Computer Networks and Cyber Security. Springer Science and Business Media LLC.
29. Gupta, B. B., and Sheng, Quan Z. (Eds.). (2019). Machine Learning for Computer and Cyber Security: Principle, Algorithms, and Practices. CRC Press.
30. B. Gupta and M. Chhabra, "A novel solution to handle DDOS attack in MANET," *Journal of Information Security*, vol. 4, no. 3, pp. 165–179, 2013.
31. R. Zhong and G. Yue, "DDoS detection system based on data mining," in Proceedings of the 2nd International Symposium on Networking and Network Security, Jinggangshan, China, 2010, pp. 2–4.
32. L. Li and G. Lee, "DDoS attack detection and wavelets," *Telecommun. Syst.*, vol. 28, no. 3–4, pp. 435–451, 2005.
33. J. Seo, C. Lee, T. Shon, K.-H. Cho, and J. Moon, "A new DDoS detection model using multiple SVMs and TRA," in International Conference on Embedded and Ubiquitous Computing, 2005, pp. 976–985.
34. K. Lee, J. Kim, K. H. Kwon, Y. Han, and S. Kim, "DDoS attack detection method using cluster analysis," *Expert Syst. Appl.*, vol. 34, no. 3, pp. 1659–1665, 2008.
35. J. Yu, H. Lee, M.-S. Kim, and D. Park, "Traffic flooding attack detection with SNMP MIB using SVM," *Comput. Commun.*, vol. 31, no. 17, pp. 4212–4219, 2008.
36. K. Hwang, P. Dave, and S. Tanachaiwiwat, "NetShield: Protocol anomaly detection with datamining against DDoS attacks," in Proceedings of the 6th International Symposium on Recent Advances in Intrusion Detection, Pittsburgh, PA, 2003, pp. 8–10.
37. H. Rahmani, N. Sahli, and F. Kammoun, "Joint entropy analysis model for DDoS attack detection," in 2009 Fifth International Conference on Information Assurance and Security, 2009, vol. 2, pp. 267–271.
38. R. Thomas, B. Mark, T. Johnson, and J. Croall, "NetBouncer: client-legitimacy-based high-performance DDoS filtering," in Proceedings DARPA Information Survivability Conference and Exposition, 2003, vol. 1, pp. 14–25.
39. L. Limwiwatkul and A. Rungsawang, "Distributed denial of service detection using TCP/IP header and traffic measurement analysis," in *Proc. IEEE Int. Symp. Communications and Information Technology*, Sapporo, Japan, 2004, October 26–29, pp. 605–610.
40. J. Wang, R. C.-W. Phan, J. N. Whitley, and D. J. Parish, "Augmented attack tree modeling of distributed denial of services and tree based attack detection method," in 2010 10th IEEE International Conference on Computer and Information Technology, 2010, pp. 1009–1014.
41. T. M. Gil and M. Poletto, "MULTOPS: A Data-Structure for Bandwidth Attack Detection," in USENIX Security Symposium, 2001, pp. 23–38.
42. K. Lu, D. Wu, J. Fan, S. Todorovic, and A. Nucci, "Robust and efficient detection of DDoS attacks for large-scale internet," *Comput. Networks*, vol. 51, no. 18, pp. 5036–5056, 2007.
43. Z. Guangsen, M. Parashar, and others, "Cooperative defence against DDoS attacks," *J. Res. Pract. Inf. Technol.*, vol. 38, no. 1, p. 69, 2006.

44. S. Kent and R. Atkinson, "Security architecture for the internet protocol," RFC 2401, November, 1998.
45. S. Kent and R. Atkinson, "IP authentication header," RFC 2402, November, 1998.
46. P. Ferguson and D. Senie, " Network ingress filtering: defeating denial of service attacks which employ IP source address spoofing," RFC 2827, 2000.
47. S. Abdelsayed, D. Glimsholt, C. Leckie, S. Ryan, and S. Shami, "An efficient filter for denial-of-service bandwidth attacks," in GLOBECOM'03. IEEE Global Telecommunications Conference (IEEE Cat. No. 03CH37489), 2003, vol. 3, pp. 1353–1357.
48. A. John and T. Sivakumar, "Ddos: Survey of traceback methods," *Int. J. Recent Trends Eng.*, vol. 1, no. 2, p. 241, 2009.
49. R. Chen, J.-M. Park, and R. Marchany, "NISp1-05: RIM: Router interface marking for IP traceback," in IEEE Globecom 2006, 2006, pp. 1–5.
50. B. Al-Duwairi and M. Govindarasu, "Novel hybrid schemes employing packet marking and logging for IP traceback," *IEEE Trans. Parallel Distrib. Syst.*, vol. 17, no. 5, pp. 403–418, 2006.
51. L. Cheng, D. M. Divakaran, W. Y. Lim, & V. Thing, U.S. Patent Application No. 16/087,625, 2019.
52. S. Suresh and N. Sankar Ram, "Enhanced deterministic packet marking mechanism for improving performance in scalability when identify attack source," *Journal of Computational and Theoretical Nanoscience*, vol. 16, no. 5–6, pp. 1956–1960, 2019.
53. O. W. Salami, I. J. Umoh, E. A. Adedokun, and M. B. Muazu, "Implementing flash event discrimination in IP traceback using shark smell optimisation algorithm," *Kinetik: Game Technology, Information System, Computer Network, Computing, Electronics, and Control*, vol. 4, no. 3, pp. 259–268, 2019.
54. J. B. D. Cabrera et al., "Proactive detection of distributed denial of service attacks using mib traffic variables-a feasibility study," in 2001 IEEE/IFIP International Symposium on Integrated Network Management Proceedings. Integrated Network Management VII. Integrated Management Strategies for the New Millennium (Cat. No. 01EX470), 2001, pp. 609–622.
55. S. Suresh and N. S. Ram, "Feasible ddos attack source traceback scheme by deterministic multiple packet marking mechanism," *The Journal of Supercomputing*, vol. 76, no. 6, pp. 4232–4246, 2020.
56. P. Fazio, M. Tropea, M. Voznak, and F. De Rango, "On packet marking and Markov modeling for IP Traceback: A deep probabilistic and stochastic analysis," *Computer Networks*, 107464, 2020.
57. Y. Kim, W. C. Lau, M. C. Chuah, and H. J. Chao, "Packetscore: Statistics-based overload control against distributed denial-of-service attacks," in IEEE INFOCOM *2004*, 2004, vol. 4, pp. 2594–2604.
58. Shah, S. B. I., Anbar, M., Al-Ani, A., & Al-Ani, A. K. (2019). "Hybridizing entropy-based mechanism with adaptive threshold algorithm to detect RA flooding attack in ipv6 networks," in Computational Science and Technology (pp. 315–323). Springer, Singapore.
59. A. T. Mizrak, S. Savage, and K. Marzullo, "Detecting compromised routers via packet forwarding behavior," *IEEE Netw.*, vol. 22, no. 2, pp. 34–39, 2008.

60. L. Zhou, H. Guo, and G. Deng, "A fog computing-based approach to DDoS mitigation in IIoT systems," *Computers & Security*, vol. 85, pp. 51–62, 2019.
61. C. Papadopoulos, R. Lindell, J. Mehringer, A. Hussain, and R. Govindan, "Cossack: Coordinated suppression of simultaneous attacks," in Proceedings DARPA Information Survivability Conference and Exposition, 2003, vol. 1, pp. 2–13.
62. Gulihar, P.and Gupta, B. B. (2020). "Cooperative Mechanisms for Defending Distributed Denial of Service (DDoS) Attacks," in Handbook of Computer Networks and Cyber Security (pp. 421–443). Springer, Cham.
63. W. Li, S. Tug, W. Meng, and Y. Wang, "Designing collaborative blockchained signature-based intrusion detection in IoT environments," *Future Generation Computer Systems*, vol. 96, pp. 481–489, 2019.
64. A. Furfaro, P. Pace, and A. Parise, "Facing DDoS bandwidth flooding attacks," *Simulation Modelling Practice and Theory*, vol. 98, p. 101984, 2020.
65. R. Mahajan, S. M. Bellovin, S. Floyd, J. Ioannidis, V. Paxson, and S. Shenker, "Controlling high bandwidth aggregates in the network," *ACM SIGCOMM Comput. Commun. Rev.*, vol. 32, no. 3, pp. 62–73, 2002.
66. D. K. Y. Yau, J. C. S. Lui, F. Liang, and Y. Yam, "Defending against distributed denial-of-service attacks with max-min fair server-centric router throttles," *IEEE/ACM Trans. Netw.*, vol. 13, no. 1, pp. 29–42, 2005
67. R. Chen and J.-M. Park, "Attack Diagnosis: Throttling distributed denial-of-service attacks close to the attack sources," in Proceedings. 14th International Conference on Computer Communications and Networks, ICCCN 2005, 2005, pp. 275–280.
68. K. Argyraki and D. R. Cheriton, "Scalable network-layer defense against internet bandwidth-flooding attacks," *IEEE/ACM Trans. Netw.*, vol. 17, no. 4, pp. 1284–1297, 2009.
69. R. Xu, Y. Chen, E. Blasch, and G. Chen, "Exploration of blockchain-enabled decentralized capability-based access control strategy for space situation awareness," *Optical Engineering*, vol. 58, no. 4, p. 041609.
70. T. Llansó, M. McNeil, and C. Noteboom, "Multi-Criteria Selection of Capability-Based Cybersecurity Solutions," in Proceedings of the 52nd Hawaii International Conference on System Sciences, 2019, January.
71. W. Wang, Q. Chen, X. He, and L. Tang, "Cooperative anomaly detection with transfer learning-based hidden markov model in virtualized network slicing," *IEEE Communications Letters*, vol. 23, no. 9, pp. 1534–1537, 2019.
72. X. Liu, X. Yang, and Y. Lu, "To filter or to authorize: Network-layer DoS defense against multimillion-node botnets," in Proceedings of the ACM SIGCOMM 2008 conference on Data communication, 2008, pp. 195–206.
73. X. L. A. L. X. Yang and D. Wetherall, "Passport: Secure and adoptable source authentication."
74. J. Mirkovic, P. Reiher, and M. Robinson, "Forming alliance for DDoS defense," in New Security Paradigms Workshop, 2003, pp. 18–21.
75. M. S. Kang, V. D. Gligor, V. Sekar, et al., "SPIFFY: Inducing cost-detectability tradeoffs for persistent link-flooding attacks," in NDSS, 2016.

Taxonomy of Economical Solutions

4

A few research works exist in this economic domain, yet this is a whole new environment where attackers are being forced to assert their validity through some analytical work. Such approaches work against the DDoS attacks in a mutual and distributive way. Several facets of an economic approach are the implementation of multiple payment systems, rational allocation of resources, enforcement of fines, competitive resource prices, complex negotiation between costs, and types of resources. Cybersecurity economics (also called information technology economics) uses the concepts of economics to explore cybersecurity. Such concepts include trade-offs faced by industry actors, undertaken under budget constraints. This domain particularly explores the economic concepts and behavioral analysis to study cybersecurity. Therefore, this chapter illuminates significant economic solutions in cyber economics. Further, it discusses some major pricing schemes on the Internet to incentivise the users to send their data wisely into the network.

4.1 CYBERSECURITY ECONOMICS

The link between the fields of computer science and economics is traced in the literature, where it has been observed that the data breach is mostly due to the presence of disproportionate incentives rather than the absence of sufficient technological protections [1]. Many of the problems exist in terms of obligation and liability for data breaches due to misallocated costs [2]. Table 4.1 shows some of the significant research works in this domain.

Now, we will discuss the pricing strategies and incentivised solutions that prevent users from misbehaving on the Internet.

TABLE 4.1   Significant works in economics of cybersecurity.

METHODOLOGY	DESCRIPTION	SIGNIFICANT PAPERS
Behavioural Analysis		
Behavioural cyberattack analysis	• One paper performs an existing botnet infiltration for the analysis of malware conversions. Other work focuses on the psychological attributes of computer scammers or the application of cybercrime analysis (forum interviews of card fraudsters).	[3–6]
Data violations	• This scientific work applies to the violations of a user's private data modelled in the laboratory.	[7]
Decision-making	• This work uses experiments to investigate the behaviour of a user towards security decisions or the response of a user to the Internet security.	[8–11]
Study on Victim		
Monitoring consumer responses/security flaws	• These studies concentrate on the experiences and reactions of users to cybercrime and polls of people who are vulnerable to phishing.	[12, 13]
The psychological impact of identity theft	• This work uses discussions/surveys to analyse the dynamics of identity fraud and the psychological and financial effect on victims.	[14, 15]
Game Theory-based Solutions		
Security investment approaches	• These papers analyse interdependent security problems and characterise rational player equilibriums.	[16, 17]
Cyber insurance models	• Such works examine how cyber insurance impacts IT protection and health of a player, including the requirements for selecting an appropriate insurance. We also examine other risk-sharing frameworks among players.	[18, 19]

Models for information sharing and data exchange	• Such studies concentrate on how to enhance safety by exchanging information on critical occurrences among contenders.	[20, 21]
Attacker-defender models	• Total effort game: Program stability relies on all participant collective effort. • Best shot game: Security of a network depends on the maximum effort employed by the participant. • Weakest player game: Security of a system depends on the effort put by the weakest participant in the network. • Network cyber-economics game.	[22, 23]
Botnet economics	• This study formulates the economic models of botnets, i.e., the black-market economy, where there is a demand and supply of compromised systems and malware services.	[24, 25]

Advancements in Methodology

Cybercrime assessment	• This study concentrates on the empirical issue of how cybercrime is assessed and quantified.	[26]

Other Research

Alerts and asset values of data breach	• These works examine the consequences of announced data breach on the market prices of an organisation.	[27]

4.1.1 Pricing Strategies

A defined objective in networking is to cohere all telecommunications services, i.e., voice, video, and data into a common IP platform. This IP platform should be able to meet the different performance standards of a range of applications envisioned, which imply advancements to the best effort service of the current Internet. This platform can be developed by exploring protocols and mechanisms of minimal QoS. Such network must employ pricing schemes that corroborate return on investment for the service providers and sustain as simple and transparent to the end users [28]. Further, Internet traffic pricing can be a reliable solution to the DDoS attacks because it can provide an appropriate QoS during congestion times for heterogeneous applications. An appropriate pricing of resources renders resource allocation problem distributed, i.e., decentralised. However, there always exist disadvantages with some advantages. The major drawback of this pricing scheme lies in the fact that it requires specialised software and hardware for traffic metering and billing process [29]. The primary purpose of any price structure is to make the best use of the available resources and to provide the best possible service to the end user.

During the early 1990s, Cocchi et al. [30] made the first attempt to address the issue of Internet charging and pricing. In 1994, MacKie-Mason and Varian [31] conceived the concept of utilisation of auction frameworks for a best-effort network in "smart businesses." This work provided the baseline for the introduction of externalities and congestion rates to the Internet. In 1995, Shenker [32] proposed an essential concept focused on a consolidated service model that incorporated both soft and hard-guaranteed services to the users. So, these are some of the initial works that introduced the pricing concept to the Internet users. Now, we will discuss some major pricing schemes.

4.1.1.1 Best effort service-based pricing

From an economic point of view, one user's usage of a network manifests undesirable externalities for others, i.e., his/her network traffic could cause delays due to congestion or loss of packets or unavailability of resources for the other users. Therefore, such a user is supposed to pay for the negative externality he is causing to the other users due to his presence in the network [33]. Generally, when the network has enough bandwidth, then the marginal cost of sending extra data packets to the network is negligible. Therefore, we focus on the pricing schemes during non-congestion times (Figure 4.1). Figure 4.1 shows the taxonomy of basic pricing strategies on Internet. Now, we will discuss some of the important best effort service-based pricing schemes.

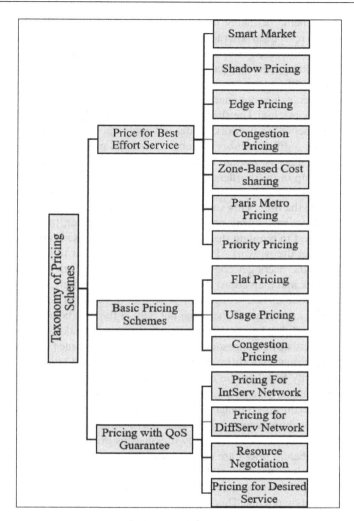

FIGURE 4.1   Taxonomy of pricing schemes on the Internet.

- Smart market pricing: Smart market [31] is a sort of congestion-pricing scheme where the header of every packet has a 'price' field to illustrate how much the sender is prepared to pay for transmitting it. The packet will be approved if the bid meets the actual transitional marginal cost mentioned by every router on the path. The consumers do not necessarily pay the price of the bid, but rather the market-clearing price representing the value of the packet accepted with the lowest priority.

This scheme definitely facilitates the service providers to generate enough revenue in order to make their business budget balance. In this case, Internet users have clear incentive to bid their value truthfully for transmitting their data packets. This scheme guarantees optimal distribution of resources among users and ensures network performance. However, it does not guarantee absolute QoS for the users.

- Shadow pricing: The shadow pricing scheme [34] is suggested and implemented to network model in which a node is able to accommodate a given number of equal sized data packets for each time frame. This is similar to fair pricing scheme. Each packet that shows up in overburdened slots gets labelled, held liable for small fixed amount called a "shadow price", and then the label is reverted back to the user. This shadow price increases at congestion hours, and decreases during non-congested hours. Further, the users are supposed to regulate their traffic after getting these marked packets from the network. This the main advantage of this scheme is where the users get cognizant about the resource statistics in the network and then adjust their sending rate accordingly.

- Edge pricing: Real congestion pricing is difficult, as computations require knowledge of the usage not only of the user being billed but also of all those users that may be impacted by the additional traffic, i.e., calculate the congestion effects along the entire route [32]. Usually, packets may take different routes situationally, and charging users arbitrarily based on the route taken by their respective data packets is just unfair because the users cannot control routing decision. This is the main disadvantage of edge pricing that the users are charged based on the anticipated congestion and short-term congestion history. This problem can be solved by making this pricing scheme centralised, wherein prices are calculated at the edge router of the service provider's network rather than making it distributed where every other access point is programmed for metering and billing.

- Congestion pricing: This pricing has been proposed to incentivise the users to shift their time of sending data from congested to non-congested slots [35]. This would help service providers to balance the load over the network. Customers are offered options to accept a congestion discount rate and switch to a following non-peak slot, or to refuse the discount bid and receive the service at a higher price immediately.

- Zone-based cost sharing: In this pricing mechanism, Clark [36] has proposed to have shared payment between the users and the service provider. This scheme is based on the assumption that it is very unfair to charge all from users or from service providers. To resolve this issue, the author has proposed an additional field in IP packet, where a user shows his willingness to pay for the service. A user will get a better service than the best effort service if he indicates his willingness; otherwise, he would get the best effort service. In this scheme, Internet is assumed to be divided into different zones where services are provided uniformly irrespective of distance. A user can choose his zone based on his requirements.

• Priority pricing: This pricing scheme has been proposed by Cocchi et al. [37] to provide multi-service levels over the best effort network. In priority-based pricing schemes, data packets are mapped into various priority levels, which would help in retaining service distinction. Traffic can be classified into different priority levels either on the basis of application or by exploring Type of Service (ToS) field in IP packet. During the time of congestion, packets having higher priority are given preference and processed with less delay. It might be the case that after paying for priority class, a user may end up with the best effort service due to the congestion in the priority class. In [38], authors have proposed a priority scheme, wherein prices get constantly updated according to the congestion and traffic load of the system.

• Paris metro pricing: In [39], Odlyzko has proposed a pricing scheme inspired from the metro system of Paris. In Paris metro network, two types of cars were offered that were identical w.r.t. seating arrangement and arrival time. However, people preferred first class and were ready to pay twice as much as the second class because they knew first class was less over-crowded. Odlyzko has stated that this self-regulation can be imposed on the Internet pricing as well. His idea was to divide Internet into different channels where every channel possesses different capacity. These channels will charge users according to their usage as users choosing higher-priced channel will have to pay more than the other users. The downside of this scheme is that deployment on the network is simple and a degree of network security and resource control is accomplished.

In the Tirupati pricing system, Dube et al. [40] have suggested something similar, in which consumers pay different rates for entering different queues that are served in a round-robin fashion by the same server.

4.1.1.2 Basic pricing schemes

The appropriate selection of an Internet pricing approach will affect the resource requirements of a user and its consumption to a significant degree that would eventually lead to improved utilisation of resources. Table 4.2 shows the basic pricing models on the Internet.

TABLE 4.2 Basic pricing schemes

PRICING STRATEGY	FEATURES	DEMERITS
Flat pricing [41]	• It is obsolete nowadays as Internet has become much overcrowded and complex place. • It can easily be applied on the users. • Consumers have to pay a fixed fee, regardless of access rate and system consumption. • There are no operational costs for billing and audit.	• This scheme has become flawed due to continuous growth in the technological advancements on the Internet. • The fairness and QoS are not guaranteed. • This scheme results in degradation of network performance as organisations lack motivation to upgrade their infrastructure.
Usage-based pricing [42]	• It is unbiased and efficient of resources utilisation. • This is effective than flat pricing. • There exists budget balance for ISPs as they can generate revenue to run their business. • It employs supply-demand paradigm where usage and price get merged.	• The peak time congestion is not addressed by this scheme. • There exist operational costs of billing and audit. • It can disincentivise users from using the Internet. • There is privacy violation in audits. • Users are charged irrespective of congestion in the network. • In P2P networks, this scheme does not fit well as P2P network is known for content sharing resulting into increased use of resources. • It is not beneficial for revenue model on the Internet.

Congestion-based pricing	• It represents the effect of individual's traffic on the performance of the network.	• There exist an overhead of fixing threshold amount periodically.
	• Generally, negative externality is imposed on the other users who send less volume of traffic into the network. This scheme alleviates this negative externality.	
	• This scheme assesses prices according to the traffic load.	
	• Various variants of this scheme, namely, shadow pricing [43] and congestion discount pricing [44], have utilised this scheme as baseline model. These schemes tend to shift the time of sending data from peak time to non-peak time.	

4.1.1.3 Pricing schemes for QoS guarantee

There has been tremendous research into the multi-level QoS on the Internet to provide a better experience to the users, and to upgrade the network performance and resource utilisation. [30] and [37] were the first attempts in establishing relations between QoS distinction and pricing. The integrated service (IntServ) is the landmark technology, wherein the Internet is integrated with the QoS capabilities. This technology has set a new paradigm, where requirements of real-time applications have met while sustaining the IP model of the Internet. Unlike IntServ networks, DiffServ defined per-hop behavior of the network. Though, it has overcome the scalability and complexity issues of IntServ network, it does not provide the complete solution for the end to end QoS management. Now, we will discuss the significant pricing schemes that guarantee QoS in the network.

- Pricing schemes for IntServ network: IntServ network usually focuses on resource reservation for every data flow using the Resource Reservation Protocol (RSVP). In [45], authors have proposed a pricing scheme using the RSVP architecture for IntServ network. This scheme utilises PATH and RESV messages of the RSVP architecture to spread the pricing information. The main limitations to this pricing system are attributed to the RSVP's own implementation challenges such as technological inconsistency and accuracy of charges imposed. In another paper [46], a protocol for attributing, charging, and tracking the available resources has been proposed. Two models have been utilised to validate this pricing scheme. The two models are auction-based model and volume-based pricing model. In the first pricing model, the bid field is integrated with the RESV message, while second model is sensitive towards congestion. The main disadvantage of this scheme is that the employment of IntServ on the internet induces lots of complexity, cost, and scalability issues.
- Pricing schemes for DiffServ network: DiffServ network is developed by Internet Engineering Task Force (IETF), where differentiated service based on the QoS levels are guaranteed. In this mechanism, multiple data flows are aggregated and processed at the edge routers with the help of information based on the resource reservation. IP packet has a field, named Differentiated Service (DS), which stores this aggregated information, named Differentiated Service Code Point (DSCP). Therefore, the internal routers are programmed to route the packets according to the DSCP information. The pricing schemes based on the DiffServ network usually work on Service Level Agreement (SLA). Table 4.3 shows the pricing schemes for DiffServ network.

TABLE 4.3 Pricing schemes for DiffServ network

AUTHOR	METHOD USED	REMARKS
Fankhauser and Plattner [46]	SLA trader	• The authors have proposed a negotiation scheme between the ISPs through bandwidth broker. • The main advantage of this scheme is that the ISPs under a contract (SLA) can share their resources with the peer ISPs. The resources can be owned by itself or purchased from another neighboring ISP. • There is no policy for charging users in DiffServ network.
Wang and Schulzrinne [47]	Long-term demand-based congestion sensitive pricing model	• The authors have proposed an optimised mechanism amalgamation of resource allocation and access control. • Congestion can be removed to a great extent while ensuring QoS levels if congestion-driven pricing is led by rate limiting methods. • Complexity is the main disadvantage of this scheme as every router on the path must be a part of this.
Semret et al. [48]	Sender pay model	• A distributed auction-based mechanism has been proposed to impose users with allocated bandwidth in a DiffServ network. • Game theory is used to define actions of broker, users and bandwidth seller in a double-layered market model. • The main advantage is that efficient allocation of bandwidth among the end users is due to strong competition among the bandwidth brokers. • A uniform SLA is prevailed across the whole network due to dynamic allocation of bandwidth at the boundary of the network.

- Pricing based on resource negotiation: Wang and Schulzrinne [49] have proposed Resource Negotiation And Pricing (RNAP) protocol, where the users are empowered to negotiate with the service provider on various QoS parameters, namely, maximum delay, peak rate, and loss rate. In this mechanism, authors have introduced provisions for centralised as well as distributed implementation of this protocol. The RNAP establishes negotiation time slots for maintaining resource reservation. A negotiation time slot defines the duration for which the contract and the price remain valid. The charge imposed on the user comprises three types of charges, namely, holding, usage, and congestion charge. Customers will pay a holding charge if they do not completely use the contractual services measured at a lower cost of service quality than the amount negotiated. The usage charge is quantified using the amount of traffic send by the user and the price per unit of data traffic during the charging cycle. Customers have to pay the congestion price if their traffic is passing across the congested network lines.

- Pricing for desired service: In the pricing schemes for desired service [50], the users are actually charged for the service they receive from the service provider. The users are charged according to the bandwidth consumption, momentary demand for bandwidth, and prioritised service a user receive for bandwidth and buffer resources. Data traffic is divided into various service classes and a user has to specify its service class before transmitting his data. If the router's buffer gets full, then the lowest priority packets are dropped; otherwise, newly arrived packets are dropped. The billing of transmission is carried out through a field in IP header, where every router adds its price based on the bandwidth and buffer resources consumption and preferential service delivered. Once this packet reaches to the destination, this total price is copied in the acknowledgement and sent back to the user. The user can adjust his sending data rate or can choose appropriate service class according to his recent payment history. Figure 4.2 shows the research scope for Internet pricing schemes. Table 4.4 shows a comparative analysis of the various pricing schemes.

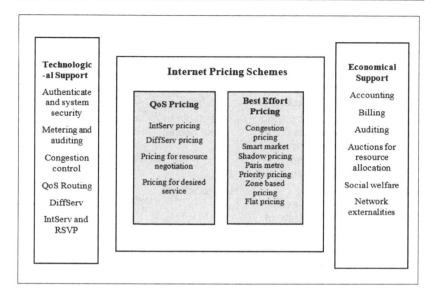

FIGURE 4.2   Range for internet pricing schemes.

4.2 CHALLENGES IN PRICING SCHEMES

Amid recent improvements in the available pricing schemes, a major issue remains that network congestion is always caused by the self-interested and rational actions of a customer. In all limited-resource networks, one participant's use of a network can adversely impact the network's attributes to others. Those consequences may include temporary congestion, and even packets loss, which is pretty evident for interactive real-time traffic. The Internet creates no incentive for the users in its current best-effort structure [51]. Further, connection duration-based pricing schemes generate no incentives for the users to take the availability of resources into account. In a packet switched network, connection duration and resource consumption are related in a non-linear fashion.

Moreover, there is an exponential growth in the various applications having different QoS and traffic requirements. The pricing schemes of the Internet must be groomed in such a way that they can easily and efficiently cope with these data-intensive, real-time and highly interactive applications.

TABLE 4.4   Comparison of various pricing schemes

PRICING SCHEME	PRICE TIME SCALE	PREDICTABILITY	SERVICE STABILITY
Smart market	The price oscillates with each packet.	Non-transparent and uncertain	Improbable and no guarantee
Edge pricing	Dynamic pricing depends on the network state and anticipation.	Predictable to some degree	No stability
Shadow pricing	The price fluctuates due to the state of the network.	Unpredictable	No stability
Zone-based cost sharing	The price oscillates with each packet.	Predictable	No stability
Priority pricing	Depends on the real-time implementation.	Depends on the real-time implementation	No stability
Paris metro	Static over longer duration.	Predictable	No stability
Congestion discount	Dynamic pricing depends on the network state and anticipation.	Predictable	No stability
IntServ	Dynamic in the contract period	Unpredictable	Stability during contract period, but no stability in re-negotiation slot.
Pricing for desired service	Works according to the network state	Unpredictable	No stability
RNAP	Dynamicity according to the negotiation between the user and the service provider.	Predictable	Stability during contract period, but no stability in re-negotiation slot.

Flat rate or congestion-based pricing cannot support such a variety of applications resulting into unfair distribution of resources and prices. Moreover, there is no clear indication as to whether the data senders or receivers should pay. The ubiquity of undesirable commercial e-mail, i.e., spam is a serious problem on the Internet today, which increases the data traffic unnecessarily [52]. A pricing system in which senders pay the full price is looking promising initially as an inexpensive and easy solution to the spam problem. Yet the simplified implementation of such a strategy will have a deterrent impact on free (or highly discounted) service suppliers of the Internet.

4.3 CHAPTER SUMMARY

In this chapter, various Internet pricing schemes have been discussed along with their advantages and disadvantages. A realistic price system would be a trade-off among technological performance, economic productivity, and social welfare. A simple, low-cost, and easily deployable scheme with modest economic efficiency is favored against a scheme with optimum economic efficiency but complicated and expensive deployment. Most of the models analysed here are of theoretical or hypothetical nature rather than practical nature. So, it's hard to make straightforward and accurate conclusions of their merit.

REFERENCES

1. Anderson, R. "Why information security is hard—An economic perspective." In *Proceedings of the 17th Annual Computer Security Applications Conference.* New Orleans, LA, 2001.
2. Moore, David, and Shannon, Colleen. "Code-Red: A case study on the spread and victims of an Internet worm." Proceedings of the 2nd ACM SIGCOMM Workshop on Internet measurement. ACM, 2002.
3. Nagurney, A., Yu, M., Masoumi, A. H., & Nagurney, L. S. (2013). *Networks against time: Supply chain analytics for perishable products.* Springer Science & Business Media.
4. Bohme, R., & Moore, T. (2010). The iterated weakest link. *IEEE Security & Privacy, 8*(1), 53–55.
5. Laszka, A., Johnson, B., & Grossklags, J. (2018). On the assessment of systematic risk in networked systems. *ACM Transactions on Internet Technology (TOIT), 18*(4), 1–28.

6. Varian, H. (2004). System reliability and free riding. In *Economics of information security* (pp. 1–15). Springer, Boston, MA.
7. Feri, L., Nijssen, S. J. J., Baggen, C. P. M. J., Gritti, T., Rajagopalan, R., De Bruijn, F. J., & Yang, H. (2016). U.S. Patent No. 9, 386, 643. Washington, DC: U.S. Patent and Trademark Office.
8. Rosoff, H., Cui, J., & John, R. S. (2013). Heuristics and biases in cyber security dilemmas. *Environment Systems and Decisions, 33*(4), 517–529.
9. Caputo, F., Scuotto, V., Carayannis, E., & Cillo, V. (2018). Intertwining the internet of things and consumers' behaviour science: Future promises for businesses. *Technological Forecasting and Social Change, 136*, 277–284.
10. Li, Q., Meng, S., Zhang, S., Hou, J., & Qi, L. (2019). Complex attack linkage decision-making in edge computing networks. *IEEE Access, 7*, 12058–12072.
11. Uslu, B., Eren, T., Gür, Ş., & Özcan, E. (2019). Evaluation of the difficulties in the internet of things (IoT) with multi-criteria decision-making. *Processes, 7*(3), 164.
12. Novak, T. P., & Hoffman, D. L. (2019). Relationship journeys in the internet of things: A new framework for understanding interactions between consumers and smart objects. *Journal of the Academy of Marketing Science, 47*(2), 216–237.
13. Nussbaum, B., & Sebastian Udoh, E. (2020). Surveillance, surveillance studies, and cyber criminality. *The Palgrave Handbook of International Cybercrime and Cyberdeviance*, 155–182.
14. Golladay, K., & Holtfreter, K. (2017). The consequences of identity theft victimization: An examination of emotional and physical health outcomes. *Victims & Offenders, 12*(5), 741–760.
15. Li, Y., Yazdanmehr, A., Wang, J., & Rao, H. R. (2019). Responding to identity theft: A victimization perspective. *Decision Support Systems, 121*, 13–24.
16. Akinwumi, D. A., Iwasokun, G. B., Alese, B. K., & Oluwadare, S. A. (2017). A review of game theory approach to cyber security risk management. *Nigerian Journal of Technology, 36*(4), 1271–1285.
17. Hyder, B., & Govindarasu, M. "Optimization of cybersecurity investment strategies in the smart grid using game-theory." In 2020 *IEEE Power & Energy Society Innovative Smart Grid Technologies Conference (ISGT)* (pp. 1–5). IEEE, 2020, February.
18. Mukhopadhyay, A., Chatterjee, S., Bagchi, K. K., Kirs, P. J., & Shukla, G. K. (2019). Cyber risk assessment and mitigation (CRAM) framework using logit and probit models for cyber insurance. *Information Systems Frontiers, 21*(5), 997–1018.
19. Radanliev, P., De Roure, D., Cannady, S., Montalvo, R. M., Nicolescu, R., & Huth, M. (2018). Economic impact of IoT cyber risk-analysing past and present to predict the future developments in IoT risk analysis and IoT cyber insurance.
20. Mohaisen, A., Al-Ibrahim, O., Kamhoua, C., Kwiat, K., & Njilla, L. (2017). Rethinking information sharing for actionable threat intelligence. *arXiv preprint arXiv,1702*.00548.
21. Saenger, J., Mazurczyk, W., Keller, J., & Caviglione, L. (2020). VoIP network covert channels to enhance privacy and information sharing. *Future Generation Computer Systems, 111*, 96–106.

22. Guan, P., He, M., Zhuang, J., & Hora, S. C. (2017). Modeling a multitarget attacker–defender game with budget constraints. *Decision Analysis, 14*(2), 87–107.
23. Cheung, K. F., & Bell, M. G. (2019). Attacker–defender model against quantal response adversaries for cyber security in logistics management: An introductory study. *European Journal of Operational Research,* 2019.
24. Cui, P., & Guin, U. "Countering botnet of things using blockchain-based authenticity framework." In 2019 IEEE Computer Society Annual Symposium on VLSI (ISVLSI) (pp. 598–603). IEEE, 2019, July.
25. Pijpker, J., & Vranken, H. "The role of Internet service providers in botnet mitigation." In 2016 European Intelligence and Security Informatics Conference (EISIC) (pp. 24–31). IEEE, 2016, August.
26. Hadlington, L. J. (2018). Employees' attitudes towards cyber security and risky online behaviours: An empirical assessment in the United Kingdom. *International Journal of Cyber Criminology, 12*(1), 262–274.
27. Shankar, N., & Mohammed, Z. (2020). Surviving data breaches: A multiple case study analysis. *Journal of Comparative International Management, 23*(1), 35.
28. Bhattacharya, P., & Guo, M. (2020). An incentive compatible mechanism for replica placement in peer-assisted content distribution. *International Journal of Software Science and Computational Intelligence (IJSSCI), 12*(1), 47–67.
29. Ma, B. J., Zhou, Z. L., & Hu, F. Y. (2017). Pricing mechanisms in the online peer-to-peer lending market. *Electronic Commerce Research and Applications, 26*, 119–130.
30. Cocchi, R., Shenker, S., Estrin, D., & Zhang, L. (1993). Pricing in computer networks: Motivation, formulation, and example. *IEEE/ACM Transactions on Networking, 1*(6), 614–627.
31. MacKie-Mason, J. K., & Varian, H. R. (1995). Pricing the internet. *Public Access to the Internet, 269*, 273.
32. Shenker, S., Clark, D., Estrin, D., & Herzog, S. (1996). Pricing in computer networks: Reshaping the research agenda. *ACM SIGCOMM Computer Communication Review, 26*(2), 19–43.
33. Hayel, Y., Ros, D., & Tuffin, B. "Less-than-best-effort services: Pricing and scheduling." In IEEE *INFOCOM 2004* (Vol. 1). IEEE, 2004, March.
34. Kelly, F. P. (1997). Charging and accounting for bursty connections. *Internet Economics,* 253–278.
35. Keon, N., & Anandalingam, G. A. (2005). A new pricing model for competitive telecommunications services using congestion discounts. *INFORMS Journal on Computing, 17*(2), 248–262.
36. Clark, D. "Combining Sender and Receiver Payments in the Internet," http://www.gta.ufrj.br/DiffServ/csrp-ddc.ps.gz
37. Cocchi, R., Estrin, D., Shenker, S., & Zhang, L. (1991). A study of priority pricing in multiple service class networks. *ACM SIGCOMM Computer Communication Review, 21*(4), 123–130.
38. Gupta, A., Stahl, D. O., & Whinston, A. B. (1997). Priority pricing of integrated services networks. *Internet Economics,* 323–352.
39. Odlyzko, A. "Paris metro pricing for the internet." In Proceedings of the 1st ACM conference on Electronic commerce (pp. 140–147), 1999, November.

40. Dube, P., Borkar, V. S., & Manjunath, D. "Differential join prices for parallel queues: Social optimality, dynamic pricing algorithms and application to internet pricing." In *Proceedings. Twenty-First Annual Joint Conference of the IEEE Computer and Communications Societies* (Vol. 1, pp. 276–283). IEEE, 2002, June.

41. Hande, P., Chiang, M., Calderbank, R., & Zhang, J. "Pricing under constraints in access networks: Revenue maximization and congestion management." In 2010 Proceedings IEEE INFOCOM (pp. 1–9). IEEE, 2010, March.

42. Nevo, A., Turner, J. L., & Williams, J. W. (2016). Usage-based pricing and demand for residential broadband. *Econometrica, 84*(2), 411–443.

43. Kelly, F. P., Maulloo, A. K., & Tan, D. K. (1998). Rate control for communication networks: shadow prices, proportional fairness and stability. *Journal of the Operational Research society, 49*(3), 237–252.

44. Keon, N., & Anandalingam, G. A. (2005). A new pricing model for competitive telecommunications services using congestion discounts. *INFORMS Journal on Computing, 17*(2), 248–262.

45. Fankhauser, G., Stiller, B., Vögtli, C., & Plattner, B. "Reservation-based charging in an integrated services network." In 4th INFORMS Telecommunications Conference, Boca Raton, Florida, USA (Vol. 302, pp. 305–309), 1998, March.

46. Fankhauser, G., & Plattner, B. (1999, December). Diffserv bandwidth brokers as mini-markets. In Workshop on Internet Service Quality Economics, MIT, US.

47. Wang, X., & Schulzrinne, H. (2006). Pricing network resources for adaptive applications. *IEEE/ACM Transactions on Networking, 14*(3), 506–519.

48. Semret, N., Liao, R. F., Campbell, A. T., & Lazar, A. A. (2000). Pricing, provisioning and peering: dynamic markets for differentiated Internet services and implications for network interconnections. *IEEE Journal on Selected Areas in Communications, 18*(12), 2499–2513.

49. Wang, X., & Schulzrinne, H. (1999). A Framework for Resource Negotiation and Pricing in the Internet. Technical Report, Columbia University.

50. O'Donnell, A. J., & Sethu, H. (2003). Congestion control, differentiated services, and efficient capacity management through a novel pricing strategy. *Computer Communications, 26*(13), 1457–1469.

51. Zhang, M., Gao, L., Huang, J., & Honig, M. L. (2019). Hybrid pricing for mobile collaborative Internet access. *IEEE/ACM Transactions on Networking, 27*(3), 986–999.

52. Nguyen, T. T., & Armitage, G. J. (2005). Evaluating Internet Pricing Schemes: A Three-Dimensional Visual Model. *ETRI Journal, 27*(1), 64–74.

DDoS Attacks on Various Platforms

5

The concept of DDoS attack is much generalised because this attack can be carried out at any point of network. This attack can be performed at any state of the network without waiting for a specific condition that triggers this attack. Hence, the features like easy to perform and difficult to detect have made the DDoS a preferable choice for the attackers. There does not exist any domain like cloud, grid, fog, IoT, or mobile computing that remains untouched by this attack. Every platform has its own vulnerabilities that are exploited by the attackers to perform this attack. Therefore, this chapter illustrates the DDoS attacks on various platforms like cloud computing and IoT. We will discuss vulnerabilities, issues, and challenges associated with each platform with regard to the DDoS attack. Apart from this, we will discuss some of the significant defence mechanisms on these platforms.

5.1 DDoS ATTACK AND CLOUD COMPUTING

Attackers exploit the key characteristics of cloud computing such as resource pooling, on-demand self-service, large network access, scalability, availability, and measured service to launch the devastating DDoS attack [1]. In cloud computing, the DDoS attacks are normally undertaken by flooding a vast quantity (high-rate) of malicious traffic in order to drain the resources of the victim servers [2, 3]. The detection of such attacks is relatively easier. Cloud computing is widely perceived as the newest computing paradigm that delivers various scalable and reliable applications leveraging the virtualisation technologies. Cloud computing helps organisations in increasing their availability to the end users. Moreover, it offers services on-demand irrespective of the geographical constraints. Cloud computing has drawn the interest of many research institutions as well as other companies due to its capabilities and cost-effectiveness [4]. High availability is important in cloud computing. The accessibility and availability of the cloud needs authoritative consumers to access cloud tools and facilities, depending on their demands. Threats to data confidentiality and service availability can, however, jeopardise the cloud environment due to its resource multitenancy and sharing features. The repercussions of the unavailability of cloud's services and resources can be ruinous; and this can lead to a temporary or, indeed, total collapse of the service delivery and infrastructure. The DDoS attack is one of the major security threats that challenges the availability cloud service. This is performed by draining the server's computing resources by inundating the network bandwidth, which leads inevitably to cloud services or resources being unavailable, resulting in massive economic losses. The elasticity, transparency, and vast volume of cloud data make them attractive targets for the attackers. Cloud web models inherit the shortcomings of their supporting technology, such as virtualisation, and they operate via normal Internet protocols [5]. The cloud capabilities that include the accessibility and scalability often usher in new risks that can be exacerbated by the Internet's anonymity [6]. Data confidentiality and integrity are passed to an external entity and this might leave users insecure because they no longer can control their data. Unlike traditional DDoS attacks on networks, DDoSing a cloud can cause service disruption, which might cross the conventional organisation's boundaries. This is due to the fact that data is handled by cloud service provider in cloud computing and the same physical hardware might store data of other organisations as well [7]. Therefore, scalability is considered as the biggest security issue in cloud computing paradigm.

5.1.1 Taxonomy of DDoS Attacks on Cloud Computing

Cloud computing primarily requires a range of emerging innovations such as virtualisation and service oriented architecture (SOA), which are extremely vulnerable to the various external and internal security problems that threaten the public clouds. Primarily, the DDoS attacks can be categorised into external and internal DDoS attacks. In external DDoS attack, an attacker has the potential to disrupt the service of thousands of virtual machines (VM) running on cloud by sending malicious traffic from

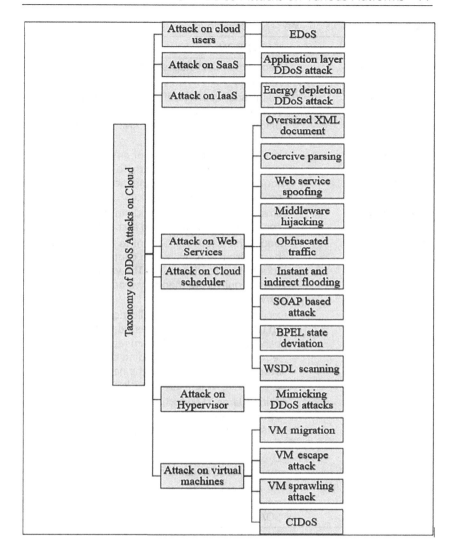

FIGURE 5.1   Taxonomy of DDoS attacks on cloud.

a botnet [8]. On the contrary, in internal DDoS attack, an attacker resides internally in the cloud and targets a group of VMs running on the same cloud. Internal DDoS attacks are more ruinous than the external ones. Figure 5.1 shows the taxonomy of DDoS attack on cloud environment. Table 5.1 shows

TABLE 5.1 Attacks on web services on cloud

ATTACK	DESCRIPTION
Port scanning	Used at the initial stages of attack. It exists in many forms like TCP ACK, TCP SYN, TCP ECHO, etc.
Coercive parsing	The intruder delivers deformed XML by adding several namespace declarations or simply by utilising very heavily nested XML constructs aimed at congesting CPU cycles.
IP spoofing	Used to fabricate the origin of a network packet in order to circumvent filters, try to conceal the source of an attack or acquire access to the protected resources or services.
User to root	Aims at obtaining rights of administrator (root) control for an unauthorised account.
Reflective attack	Request messages will be sent to reflector systems by zombie machines, which contain the victim's spoofed source IP address. The valid responses to these inquiries are then forwarded to the flooding survivor.
Flooding	Occurs via network and application layers such as HTTP, ICMP etc. It aims to inundate the network bandwidth to prohibit it from replying to the legitimate user traffic. Flooding can be direct attack by zombies against the network or application, or reflective attacks.
Large-sized XML	Multiple large XML documents containing attributes, or namespaces with large names are sent by the attacker. These documents are then parsed by Document Object Model (DOM) in its memory to check its completeness resulting in increased memory requirements by a factor of 5–30.
Web service spoofing	This is an enhanced version of the spoofing attack where the Reply To or Fault To address is faked in a SOAP header resulting in a reflective attack.

some variants of DDoS attacks that are possible on cloud computing environment. Following are the points specifying different types of DDoS attacks on cloud services and on cloud users.

- Attacks against cloud users: An SLA is the contract that regulates communication between the user and the cloud provider. This ensures that the SLA contains the services the cloud provider provides, and even includes the QoS of certain resources the customer needs from the cloud service provider (CSP) [9]. An Economic Denial of Service (EDoS) is the attack that target users as well as CSPs at the same time. In this attack, an attacker sends forged requests to the provider resulting in increased load at the server [10]. This will lead to large bills for the users. These attacks prove very critical to the SLAs as to meet the required QoS, the provider has to allocate more resources to the users during the attack period and users will have to pay the bill [11].

- Attacks on Software as a Service (SaaS): The DDoS attackers target the layer that provides software and applications as a service to the users on demand. The attackers tend to exploit the vulnerabilities present in the software and try to make them unavailable or functionless for the users. The attackers mainly use HTTP and HTTPS to launch these attacks. Moreover, these attacks are difficult to detect [12, 13].

- Attacks on Infrastructure as a Service (IaaS): Cloud infrastructures like cloud data centres can be affected by the DDoS attacks. There exists a new variant of DDoS attack, namely, energy depletion DDoS attack, where an attacker tends to keep busy target data centre in processing and serving malicious data requests resulting in consumption and wastage of lots of energy in cloud data centre [14]. Further, cloud data centres are penalised due to over-gas emissions resulting from the over-utilisation of the resources at cloud data centres [15].

- Attack on web services: There exist numerous DDoS attacks on web services in cloud computing environment. XML has been extensively used on web for encoding messages and communications between two devices. An attacker carries out coercive parsing attack on the web services by sending a SOAP message containing a large number of open tags, i.e., very complex nested XML document. Cloud server loses its lots of computing power in processing this large XML document. Over-sized XML document attack is a type of coercive attack, where XML attribute and element count are exploited.

In XML attribute and element attack, the body of SOAP consists of a large number of attributes and non-nested elements, respectively, to make the target run out of processing power. Web service spoofing attack has also been discussed in Table 5.1. Next, unlikely web service spoofing attack, in middleware hijacking attack, URLs of attackers are directed towards an existing cloud data centre [16]. The attackers tend to run a real-time service at the specified URL; therefore, web service continuously try to respond to the requests sent by the attackers. In attack obfuscation, an attacker has the capability to exploit the encryption of XML documents to camouflage the data to prevent it from being detected. This attack can be utilised to perform XML injection and oversize payload attacks. In Business Process Execution Language (BPEL) state deviation attack, an attacker exploits the BPEL engine, which is capable of providing web service with the end points to every type of service request. It runs multiple instants or threads while processing a service request. The attacker exploits these features by attacking these end points and sends large-sized message request. The BPEL engine processes the requests that have no association with currently running instance and resulting in the consumption of large resources. Instant and immediate flooding attacks are similar to the BPES state deviation attack. In SOAP-based attack, an attacker impose web service by sending large-sized SOAP messages.

- Attack on cloud scheduler: The hypervisor can monitor multiple VMs at the same time. This hypervisor has several vulnerabilities to be exploited by the attackers. These attacks result in inaccurate scheduling of VMs [17].
- Attacks on hypervisor: In such attacks, a cloud user deploys a malicious guest operating system by leasing a guest VM [18]. Instead, after activating this malicious OS, the attackers are prepared to target the hypervisor through accessing the memory contents of the adjacent VMs and modifying the hypervisor's source code. The DDoS attackers can mask their attacks in the mimicking DDoS attacks, by emulating legitimate traffic to avoid detection.
- Attack on virtual machines: Virtualisation is considered as the main feature of the cloud computing environment. This feature is utilised to run multiple VMs on a single host.

The cybersecurity risks to the physical systems are identical to the security threats that could affect the VM world [19]. When a host machine gets overloaded, then the VMs running on it are transferred to another server. This migration of VMs is a costly process. In VM migration attack, an attacker tends to exhaust the resources of VMs resulting in degraded performance of cloud environment. Inappropriate VM management procedure leads to VM sprawling attack.

5.1.2 Taxonomy of DDoS Defence Mechanisms on Cloud

Defence strategies in cloud computing can be divided mainly into three categories, namely, attack prevention, detection, and mitigation. In attack

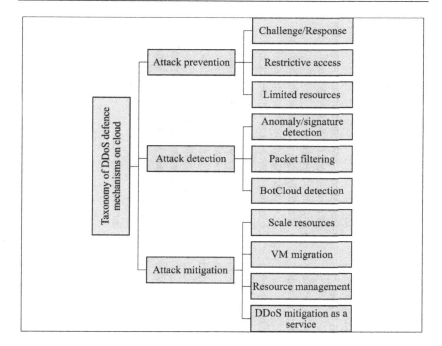

FIGURE 5.2 Taxonomy of DDoS defensive mechanisms on cloud.

prevention, pro-active measures are taken by the network to stop infiltration of malicious traffic. In attack prevention techniques, there are no traces of attack in the network and these are applicable to both legitimate and malicious users. Attack detection techniques are employed when attack traces have just started to degrade the performance of the server according to some parameter. Attack mitigation techniques will try to mitigate the effects of attack after it has been detected. Figure 5.2 shows the taxonomy of DDoS defence mechanisms on cloud.

Now, we will discuss each category briefly in the following section.

5.1.2.1 DDoS attack prevention on cloud

Restrictive access, challenge response puzzles, and hidden vulnerable ports are some of the methods that are included in attack prevention mechanisms. Table 5.2 discusses these techniques with pros and cons.

TABLE 5.2   DDoS preventive measures on cloud

METHODS	STRENGTHS	LIMITATIONS
Restrictive access [20–22]	• These techniques are utilised for admission control. • Preventive action is employed by providing delayed response or delayed access to the suspected users or the new users. • In some mechanisms, reputation of a user has also been utilised to prioritise users to provide access to the users. • These methods facilitate in optimising server's capacity according to the available resources.	• Access restriction puts constraint on server to process the service requests of the new users. • Operational costs for maintaining number of connections for delayed period. • Quality of service issues. • Scalability issue in massive and high rate DDoS attacks where attackers use IP spoofing from a large number of sources.
Challenge response [23–25]	• These methods are effectively utilised for identifying real users or bot machines. • Simply automated, bot sourced, and rate-based DDoS attacks can be identified using this method. • Cryptographic puzzle or Proof of Work (PoW) is one of the methods where a crypto puzzle needs to be solved by the user correctly and timely to prove his legitimacy. • Computational burden is shifted to the users. • Accessibility and conversion rate are two important factors which must be focused while designing a challenge response mechanism.	• Overhead of maintenance and storage of graphics generation. • Text puzzles are susceptible to dictionary attack or parsing attacks. • Prone to puzzle accumulation attack where attacker tends to send a large number of requests for puzzles, but does not solve them. This makes server exhaust a number of puzzles.

| Hidden servers or ports [26, 27] | • Hidden servers or ports have been utilised to shield server from direct communication from the attackers.
• A proxy server is kept as functioning authority. These proxies balance the load, monitor the incoming traffic for determining any anomaly, and help to recover. | • Overhead of maintaining replica servers and computational overhead of directing the traffic from one target to another. |
| Limited resources [28] | • Auto-scaling decisions can be précised by the knowledge of limited resources.
• Puts restriction on resource usage for each service.
• Helps in limiting the bills for service provider during server downtime. | • Important feature of on-demand service in cloud computing cannot render its benefits to the users and service providers as well.
• It is not effective in preventing DDoS attack, but can reduce the economic losses. |

5.1.2.2 DDoS attack detection on cloud

Anomaly and signature, packet filtering, and botcloud detection are some of the major DDoS attack detection mechanisms on cloud. Table 5.3 discusses the advantages and disadvantages of these mechanisms briefly.

5.1.2.3 DDoS attack mitigation on cloud

Resource scaling, VM migration, and DDoS mitigation as a service are some of the techniques that are covered by mitigation techniques on cloud. Table 5.4 discusses some of the important work in this sub-domain.

5.2 DDoS ATTACKS IN IoT

Past few years have witnessed some major technologies that have unveiled the various applications that the Internet could have. The IoT is one of them that has played the biggest game in this evolution. The IoT can be described as a network of interconnected objects and individuals delivering services and exchanging data to accomplish a task in various applications. The main aim of the IoT is to change our everyday lives and to mutate our way of carrying out the various activities. Its applications have very broad range, i.e., from household to industrial [45]. After its advent, the IoT has attracted considerable criticism in developing and installing its hardware, applications, and network elements for the lack of commitment extended to security matters. Such reckless approach has resulted in numerous vulnerabilities which have already been effectively abused by the hackers to manipulate the components of IoT so that they can be subverted for various purposes, i.e., for launching DDoS attacks. Attackers are moving towards technologies like IoT and mobile computing to amplify and strengthen their DDoS attacks. The IoT has an unprecedented potential for scalability and flexibility. Some of the key priorities is to ensure that adequate security mechanisms to deter any threats that may breach integrity and availability of service [45, 46]. One of the key IoT security consideration is to guarantee data availability to all the authenticated users all time. Figure 5.3 shows the DDoS attacks on the IoT.

The IoT has a dominant presence in the reports scanning the evolution of DDoS attacks after the first Mirai attack took place in 2016, owing to how easily smart devices can be hijacked. Cisco predicted the existence of about 3.5 wired devices per person by the year 2020. Global IoT investment will undergo an average cumulative growth rate of 15.6%, exceeding $1.29 trillion

TABLE 5.3 DDoS detection methods on cloud

METHODS	STRENGTHS	LIMITATIONS
Anomaly and signature detection mechanisms [29, 30]	• These mechanisms have tried to find out anomaly in traffic flow by comparing it with past behaviours or nominal profile. • A nominal web behaviour is modelled in non-attack period using several characteristics and parameters. • Machine learning and feature detection are widely used in these mechanisms. • Growth of technologies like big data analytics and Software-defined Networking (SDN) have facilitated quick attack detection using anomaly detection mechanisms.	• Behavioural analysis in terms of features and anomalies is a major issue. • IP spoofing-based DDoS attack is difficult to detect. • Minimising false alarms is a major issue.
Packet filtering [31, 32]	• These mechanisms utilise hop count or number of connections or number of requests-based threshold values to filter malicious packets. • Easy deployment and support by the already available OS-based firewalls.	• False positives and negatives are important performance issues. • IP spoofing-based DDoS attacks cannot be detected.
BotCloud detection [14, 33, 34]	• Cloud infrastructure is utilised to install bots where VMs can be compromised. • Network and VMM level monitoring has been performed to identify malicious VM. • In another work, trivial actions of malicious VMs have been stored in a database and clustering technique has been used to determine bot cloud. • Various anomaly detection approaches have also been used.	• Zero-day attacks cannot be detected by these approaches. • Setting threshold value for various suspicious activities is a major issue.
Traceback mechanisms [35, 36]	• These mechanisms help in tracking the malicious web requests to their original source IP address. • Neural network tracing, path reconstruction using SOA, OS fingerprinting, and statistical filtering to prevent IP spoofing, packet marking, TTL probing mechanisms have been used for tracking back the original sources.	• It requires cooperation from other networking entities. • Massive DDoS attack using large scale IP spoofing is difficult to detect.

TABLE 5.4 DDoS mitigation mechanisms on cloud

METHODS	STRENGTHS	LIMITATIONS
Resource scaling [37, 38]	• Resource scaling helps server remain accessible and available during the attack time. • Dynamic resource allocation schemes can contribute to this domain.	• The main disadvantage of this scheme is that if the attack goes undetected, then it might up end with huge attack costs.
VM migration [39, 40]	• This mechanism involves shifting of targeted server to other physical server without observing any downtime. • Proxy gateways or routers can also be shifted to overlay networks to prevent any disruption to the existing network.	• Sometimes, the attackers might intentionally migrate server to the other server to increase the collateral damage. • There is a wastage of extra resources to maintain another server.
DDoS mitigation as a service [41, 42]	• Outsourcing cloud security to other entity which is full dedicated towards providing DDoS mitigation as a service. • Hybrid firewalls comprise physical and virtual firewall that tends to impose caps or limits on maximum allocated resources. • Real time monitoring of metrics related to a service are some of the significant solutions in this domain.	• Remote DDoS mitigation can slow the mitigation process. • Privacy issue arises when victim cloud hires a third party to provide mitigation service.
SDN-based solutions [43, 44]	• Reconfigurability feature of SDN provides immense scope for mitigating slow rate and massive DDoS attacks. • Deep inspection of data packets utilising SDN can be an effective solution against DDoS attacks. • Strict access control policies employed by the SDN is also a good solution towards strong authentication mechanisms.	• Even SDN is susceptible to DDoS attacks. • Mostly effective at network boundaries or at ISP level.

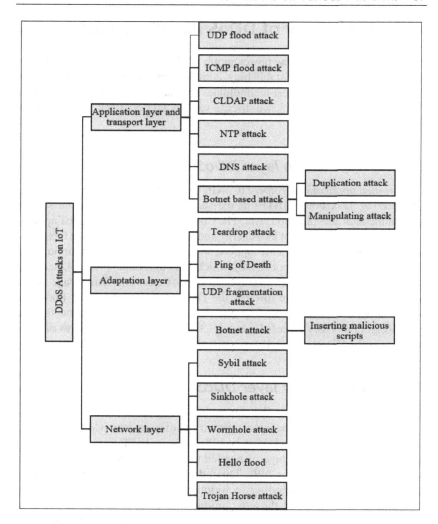

FIGURE 5.3   DDoS on IoT.

in 2020, according to the International Data Corporation (IDC) [45]. The IoT is a complex network of sensitive and inter-connected appliances, sensors, and applications, most of which have been developed while keeping security at the lowest priority [46, 47].

5.2.1 Taxonomy of DDoS Attacks on IoT

Resource constraint and low power supply of the IoT devices make them easy target for the attackers. Establishing complicated security measures on the IoT devices, given the latest technologies in place, is still continued to be a difficult task. In Figure 5.3, we discuss various DDoS attack possible in the IoT environment.

5.2.1.1 Application layer DDoS attacks

Constrained application protocol (CoAP) has been introduced by the Internet Engineering Task Force (IETF) as the standard protocol to regulate smooth communication at application layer. The CoAP is configured for the IoT applications considering features of low-energy and low-loss network such as flexibility, low operational costs, multicast support, and reduced energy consumption [48]. The User Datagram Protocol (UDP), which is an unreliable protocol, has been used to transmit the CoAP messages in the IoT network. This usage of the UDP makes it more prone towards the DDoS attacks. The UDP flood, the ICMP flood, the Domain name service (DNS) attack, and the Connectionless Lightweight Directory Access Protocol (CLDAP) attack are examples of some variants of the DDoS attacks that are possible on this platform.

5.2.1.2 Adaptation layer DDoS attacks

Adaptation layer is responsible for empowering IPv6 communications in the IoT environment. The maximum transmission unit (MTU) in IPv6 protocol is 1280 bytes, while it is 127 bytes in IEEE 802.15.4 network. Therefore, an adaptation layer is needed to generate compatibility between the two types of networks [49]. This adaptation of data packets requires header optimisation, including techniques like compression, fragmentation, and reassembly. All these techniques have made this layer prone to the DDoS attacks. Ping of death, UDP fragmentation, and tear drop attack are some possible attacks on this layer.

5.2.1.3 Network layer DDoS attacks

Routing protocol (RPL) has been introduced by the IETF in network layer to lessen energy consumption by optimising routing paths through point-to-point, point-to-multipoint etc. [50, 51]. There is no denying the fact that this RPL is susceptible to the DDoS attacks.

5.2.2 Botnet-based Attacks in IoT

The huge availability of insecure and vulnerable IoT devices fascinates attackers and they have advanced methods and tools to create a botnet out of these devices. The attackers take the advantage of the fact that these devices can be compromised remotely as well. Every infected IoT device is called bot. Now, we will discuss methods used by the attackers to generate IoT-based botnet.

- Inserting malicious code: After adeptly granting access to an IoT node, the attacker can insert malicious scripts into its memory and can control the entire IoT environment. This code is then utilised to eavesdrop the network and to hunt for new vulnerable devices.
- Trojan attack: The attacker tends to mount an activating device into the IoT device during this manufacturing. The attacker can manipulate the device or can access the data collected by it or use it to infect other devices.
- Duplication attack: An attacker generates an identical copy of the legitimate node in the IoT environment by copying data from it. Another damage done by this bogus node is that it operates as an illegitimate machine and transmits incorrect information to other connected nodes resulting in the production of incorrect data overall. This incorrect data can impact the real-time decision-making process of industries resulting in reduced productivity and performance.
- Deterioration of limited resources of IoT devices: IoT devices use low-power batteries, therefore employ sleep mode to better control the energy usage of such devices for optimal use. The device utilises its resources when activated by the IoT network; otherwise, it tends to remain in sleep mode to preserve its limited resources. An attacker exploits this functionality and forcibly makes an IoT device to skip its sleeping mode unnecessarily so that the device runs short of battery resource. This attack can be very disastrous when during an emergency situation, an IoT device has to collect sensory data and report it to the server. In medical IoT or in any nation's critical infrastructure, this attack can have serious consequences.
- Manipulating attack: When an IoT device performs the process of sensory data collection, then there is no human intervention. Moreover, these devices can be accessed remotely. These two factors make IoT devices very much prone to manipulating attacks.

5.2.3 Taxonomy of DDoS Defences in IoT

Like in cloud environment, the DDoS attack defence strategies can be divided into same three categories, namely, prevention, detection, and mitigation. Prevention techniques help defenders in stopping the identified or detected DDoS attack from getting dispersed into the whole network or stopping it at its initial stage. Now, we will discuss each of the three defence strategies in following subsections.

5.2.3.1 Attack prevention

In [52], a mutual authentication scheme has been developed for medical IoT. This scheme is based on Datagram Transport Layer Security (DTLS) handshake and is processed between the gateway and the end user. The gateway router maintains a complete list of authorised IoT devices that are permitted to interact within the IoT ecosystem. The gateway also maintains the count of number of times a node has requested to interact with other nodes and discard its requests if it crosses a certain threshold value. This scheme is able to prevent the DDoS and replay attacks. In [53], the authors have proposed a mechanism named MECshield based on the mobile edge computing. The mobile edge computing has been utilised to deploy multiple filters at the boundary of the network. A central entity monitors the communication between these intelligent filters and determines the features of the attacking or malicious traffic. In [54], the authors have proposed a machine learning-based DDoS defence strategy on an IoT platform. In this mechanism, the intrusion detection system (IDS) employs naïve Bayes classifier on multiple IoT nodes as multi-agents to prevent any instance of DDoS attacks. This mechanism is named as Naive Bayes Classifier-Multi-agent Intrusion Detection System (NBC-MAIDS). These nodes then monitor and audit the traffic and help in management of nodes. In [55], the authors have proposed MAEC-X, i.e., multi-access level edge computing, where a controller entity is located at cloud and MAEC-X users are deployed at the edge nodes and data centres. These MAEC-X entities have embedded prevention and detection module, which monitors the data traffic in real time. These entities report relevant information regarding the DDoS attack to the controller and the controller warns other nodes in the IoT network to take appropriate actions. This mechanism can prevent the ICMP and the UDP flood attacks. In [56], edge nodes have been made the first layer of security mechanism against the DDoS attacks. The cloud web service will be provided the sketch of data traffic by the edge nodes. The edge nodes monitor the legitimacy of data traffic using fastpath. This mechanism has proved to be very beneficial over the existing systems, as it has the provision for priority packet scheduling. In this provision, smaller packets are sent for self-authentication process, as they tend to travel faster than the regular data packets. In [57], the authors have proposed a TCP attack detection and prevention mechanism for cloud environment. This mechanism can be successfully applied on the IoT as Least Squares Support Vector Machine (LS-SVM); a machine learning algorithm is employed to detect and prevent any instance of a DDoS attack on the cloud. In detection phase, it will assess incoming traffic and compare it with the blacklisted log server. If the data parameters do not match with the data present in the blacklist log server, then this traffic is sent to the classifier to assess that whether the data packet is a part of the malicious traffic or not.

5.2.3.2 Attack detection

In [58], the authors have proposed a machine learning-based DDoS attack detection mechanism. A computationally low-cost algorithm is implemented on the local IoT nodes to detect the DDoS attack traffic. It utilises packet level detection policy to determine the malicious packets. In [59], a unique method of utilising network time protocol (NTP) has been proposed to defend the DDoS attacks in the IoT network. The clock of a device is always synched with the clock of the server and the overall delay in the processing of data leads to asynchronisation between the two clocks. This feature is used in this mechanism to identify the DDoS attacks. The NTP user contacts the server to find out the difference in both the clocks. The DDoS attack is detected based on this difference as its occurrence is guaranteed if the clock of the device is unable to get in line with the clock of the server. In [60], the authors have proposed a mechanism utilising bidirectional long short-term memory recurrent neural network to find botnet in the IoT environment. This method is based on the assessment of packet flow, however, unlikely other packet flow-based mechanisms, this method works on identifying the text within features. This mechanism can detect the UDP flooding and the DNS attacks with 98% accuracy. Now, we will discuss solutions that have been proposed for other platforms like cloud and SDN, but can be applied on the IoT as well. In [61], a fuzzy logic-based DDoS defence mechanism has been proposed for the cloud network. In this mechanism, firstly, all data traffic is filtered using fuzzy logic and then, allowed to enter into the cloud. The fuzzy logic system is designed using If-Else constructs, and it reports to the cloud if any discrepancy is found in the traffic. In [62], the authors have utilised deep learning techniques to detect the DDoS attacks on cloud. Recurrent Neural Network (RNN) has been used for the purpose. The authors have modelled the DDoS detection problem into sequence classification problem and converted the packet-based detection to window-based detection. The

Long Short-Term Memory (LSTM) and the Gated Recurrent Unit (GRU) Neural Network have been used to eradicate the scaling issues. In [63], a mechanism named Complex Event Processing Intrusion Detection System (CEPIDS) has been developed, where Intrusion Detection Systems (IDSs) are employed at the boundary of the network. This mechanism has enabled real-time analysis of the traffic. The responsibility of CEPIDS is to collect the data traffic through event filter. This event filter is composed of two components, namely, packet analyser and attack detection. Both modules contribute in analysing the collected traffic and to detect the DDoS attack.

5.2.3.3 Attack mitigation

In [64], the authors have proposed a honeypot-based DDoS mitigation mechanism for the IoT environment. Firstly, traffic is passed through IDS and after identified as malicious, this traffic is directed towards the honeypot, which analyses and determines the nature of the attack. If the malicious traffic appears to come from a particular IP address repeatedly by the honeypot, then that IP address will be blocked. In [65], the authors have proposed a mechanism, wherein the DDoS attack detection, intruder identification, and mitigation take place at the same time. This mechanism tends to find out the cosine similarity of vectors of every data packet rate at software-defined (SD) IoT switches. If the incoming data packet has no similarity with the flow table, then it is forwarded towards the controller. The controller traces back the actual source of this data packet. The algorithm helps in immediately determining which IoT node has been used to initiate the DDoS attacks and can be subsequently mitigated. The dynamic predictive congestion control (DPCC) algorithm has been used by the existing solutions to monitor the traffic load at SD-IoT switches, but this algorithm is unable to address such a large amount of data traffic and, hence, cannot detect the DDoS attacks. This proposed mechanism has used threshold value-based detection mechanism resulting in quicker detection of the DDoS attacks. In [66], the authors have proposed a mechanism to identify the inbuilt security of the IoT devices. They have combined machine learning and SDN to detect and mitigate the DDoS attacks and they have named it SoftThings. The SDN is employed to monitor the data traffic flow and if any discrepancy is found, it reports it to the SDN controller. Afterwards, machine learning-based support vector machine is utilised to distinguish the malicious packet flow. Once found the malicious IoT node, the SDN controller gets updated with the node so that it can prevent the node from communicating with the other nodes. In [67], the authors have studied Mirai botnet attack and proposed edge-based detection mechanism by utilising the SDN and fog computing. In a fog computing environment, security measures are deployed at edge nodes to make the security mechanism as close as possible to the IoT devices. There are two phases in this mechanism, namely, scanning and mitigating. In scanning phase, these edge nodes scan the incoming traffic and try to find out any suspicious activity. Afterwards, malicious packets are dropped according to an updated blacklist. There exist many solutions that have been proposed in different platforms, but can be effectively applied to the IoT environment. In [68], the authors have explored Network Function Virtualisation (NFV) and edge computing to mitigate the DDoS attacks. Traffic scanning takes place at the edge nodes, while NFV is used to scale resources. In [69], the authors have utilised deep learning mechanism, i.e., deep reinforcement learning, which can be self-trained according to the DDoS attack state in the network. At SDN controller, deep reinforcement learning is employed to distinguish the attack traffic and allow legitimate traffic to access the target server.

These are some of the DDoS attack preventing, detecting, and mitigating solutions that have been proposed so far. A lot of work is undertaken to handle the variants of DDoS attacks and yet an upward trend appears to be apparent. Insecurity and massiveness of the IoT devices are the two key reasons for such an exponential development. The reason behind this is most of these devices do not have the required security protocol in place to defend themselves from this hostile attack.

5.3 CHAPTER SUMMARY

In this chapter, we have studied two platforms, i.e., cloud environment and the IoT w.r.t. the DDoS attacks. A detailed study of the DDoS attacks, their taxonomy and the corresponding solutions have been discussed for cloud computing and the IoT as well. Apart from this, we have discussed inherited vulnerabilities of these platforms that are exploited by the attackers to launch several devastating attacks. Further, we have unveiled detailed categorisation of defence mechanisms for these platforms, i.e., prevention, detection, and mitigation. This study will play a significant role in providing the basis for advanced and effective approaches for stopping and deterring the DDoS attacks on the cloud and the IoT environment. In cloud environment, multi-level solutions based on cost and resource aware resource allocation algorithms work better than the conventional approaches. On the other hand, in the IoT environment, the lack of inherited security mechanisms in the IoT devices during their manufacturing is the key factor behind the occurrences of cyberattacks.

REFERENCES

1. Gonzalez, J. D. T., & Kinsner, W. (2016). Zero-crossing analysis of lévy walks and a DDoS dataset for real-time feature extraction: Composite and applied signal analysis for strengthening the internet-of-things against DDoS attacks. *International Journal of Software Science and Computational Intelligence (IJSSCI)*, *8*(4), 1–28.
2. Bhushan, K., & Gupta, B. B. (2017). Security challenges in cloud computing: state-of-art. *International Journal of Big Data Intelligence*, *4*(2), 81–107.
3. Gou, Z., Yamaguchi, S., & Gupta, B. B. (2017). Analysis of various security issues and challenges in cloud computing environment: A survey. In Identity Theft: Breakthroughs in Research and Practice (pp. 221–247). IGI Global.
4. Kumar, A. (2019). Design of secure image fusion technique using cloud for privacy-preserving and copyright protection. *International Journal of Cloud Applications and Computing (IJCAC)*, *9*(3), 22–36.
5. Somani, G., Gaur, M. S., Sanghi, D., Conti, M., & Buyya, R. (2017). DDoS attacks in cloud computing: Issues, taxonomy, and future directions. *Computer Communications*, *107*, 30–48.
6. Gupta, B. B. (2019). An efficient KP design framework of attribute-based searchable encryption for user level revocation in cloud. Concurrency and Computation: Practice and Experience, e5291.
7. Priyadarshinee, P. (2018). Cloud computing adoption: scale development, measurement and validation. *International Journal of Cloud Applications and Computing (IJCAC)*, *8*(1), 97–116.
8. Dong, S., Abbas, K., & Jain, R. (2019). A survey on distributed denial of service (DDoS) attacks in SDN and cloud computing environments. *IEEE Access*, *7*, 80813–80828.
9. VivinSandar, S., & Shenai, S. (2012). Economic denial of sustainability (EDoS) in cloud services using HTTP and XML based DDoS attacks. *International Journal of Computer Applications*, *41*(20).
10. Bhushan, K., & Gupta, B. B. (2019). Network flow analysis for detection and mitigation of Fraudulent Resource Consumption (FRC) attacks in multimedia cloud computing. *Multimedia Tools and Applications*, *78*(4), 4267–4298.
11. Monge, M. A. S., Vidal, J. M., & Pérez, G. M. (2019). Detection of economic denial of sustainability (EDoS) threats in self-organizing networks. *Computer Communications*, *145*, 284–308.
12. Aouzal, K., Hafiddi, H., & Dahchour, M. (2019). Policy-Driven Middleware for Multi-Tenant SaaS Services Configuration. *International Journal of Cloud Applications and Computing (IJCAC)*, *9*(4), 86–106.
13. Siva, T., & Krishna, E. P. (2013). Controlling various network based ADoS attacks in cloud computing environment: by using port hopping technique. *Int. J. Eng. Trends Technol*, *4*(5), 2099–2104.
14. Herzfeldt, A., Floerecke, S., Ertl, C., & Krcmar, H. (2019). Examining the antecedents of cloud service profitability. *International Journal of Cloud Applications and Computing (IJCAC)*, *9*(4), 37–65.

15. Al-Nawasrah, A., Almomani, A. A., Atawneh, S., & Alauthman, M. (2020). A survey of fast flux botnet detection with fast flux cloud computing. *International Journal of Cloud Applications and Computing (IJCAC), 10*(3), 17–53.

16. Jadad, H. A., Touzene, A., & Day, K. (2020). Offloading as a service middleware for mobile cloud apps. *International Journal of Cloud Applications and Computing (IJCAC), 10*(2), 36–55.

17. Velliangiri, S., Karthikeyan, P., & Vinoth Kumar, V. (2020). Detection of distributed denial of service attack in cloud computing using the optimization-based deep networks. *Journal of Experimental & Theoretical Artificial Intelligence*, 1–20.

18. Aldribi, A., Traoré, I., Moa, B., & Nwamuo, O. (2020). Hypervisor-based cloud intrusion detection through online multivariate statistical change tracking. *Computers & Security, 88*, 101646.

19. Morbitzer, M., Huber, M., & Horsch, J. (2019, March). Extracting secrets from encrypted virtual machines. In Proceedings of the Ninth ACM Conference on Data and Application Security and Privacy (pp. 221–230).

20. Masood, M., Anwar, Z., Raza, S. A., & Hur, M. A. (2013, December). EDoS armor: A cost effective economic denial of sustainability attack mitigation framework for e-commerce applications in cloud environments. In INMIC (pp. 37–42). IEEE.

21. Baig, Z. A., Sait, S., & Binbeshr, F. S. (2016). U.S. Patent Application No. 14/970,152.

22. Saini, B., & Somani, G. (2014, March). Index page based EDoS attacks in infrastructure cloud. In International Conference on Security in Computer Networks and Distributed Systems (pp. 382–395). Springer, Berlin, Heidelberg.

23. Alosaimi, W., & Al-Begain, K. (2013, June). A new method to mitigate the impacts of the economical denial of sustainability attacks against the cloud. In Proceedings of the 14th Annual Post Graduates Symposium on the convergence of Telecommunication, Networking and Broadcasting (PGNet) (pp. 116–121).

24. Saravanan, A., Bama, S. S., Kadry, S., & Ramasamy, L. K. (2019). A new framework to alleviate DDoS vulnerabilities in cloud computing. *International Journal of Electrical & Computer Engineering, 9*(2088–8708).

25. Gumaei, A., Sammouda, R., Al-Salman, A. M. S., & Alsanad, A. (2019). Anti-spoofing cloud-based multi-spectral biometric identification system for enterprise security and privacy-preservation. *Journal of Parallel and Distributed Computing, 124*, 27–40.

26. Jeyanthi, N., & Mogankumar, P. C. (2014). A virtual firewall mechanism using army nodes to protect cloud infrastructure from DDoS attacks. *Cybernetics and Information Technologies, 14*(3), 71–85.

27. Jia, Q., Wang, H., Fleck, D., Li, F., Stavrou, A., & Powell, W. (2014, June). Catch me if you can: A cloud-enabled DDoS defense. In *2014 44th Annual IEEE/IFIP International Conference on Dependable Systems and Networks* (pp. 264–275). IEEE.

28. Amazon Web Services, AWS best practices for DDoS resiliency, 2015, (https://d0.awsstatic.com/whitepapers/DDoS_White_Paper_June2015.pdf).

29. Rawashdeh, A., Alkasassbeh, M., & Al-Hawawreh, M. (2018). An anomaly-based approach for DDoS attack detection in cloud environment. *International Journal of Computer Applications in Technology, 57*(4), 312–324.

30. Ghosh, P., Shakti, S., & Phadikar, S. (2016). A cloud intrusion detection system using novel PRFCM clustering and KNN based dempster-shafer rule. *International Journal of Cloud Applications and Computing (IJCAC)*, *6*(4), 18–35.
31. Shidaganti, G. I., Inamdar, A. S., Rai, S. V., & Rajeev, A. M. (2020). SCEF: A model for prevention of DDoS attacks from the cloud. *International Journal of Cloud Applications and Computing (IJCAC)*, *10*(3), 67–80.
32. Khan, M. S., Ferens, K., & Kinsner, W. (2015). Multifractal singularity spectrum for cognitive cyber defence in internet time series. *International Journal of Software Science and Computational Intelligence (IJSSCI)*, *7*(3), 17–45.
33. Hammi, B., Rahal, M. C., & Khatoun, R. (2016, July). Clustering methods comparison: Application to source based detection of botclouds. In 2016 International Conference on Security of Smart Cities, Industrial Control System and Communications (SSIC) (pp. 1–7). IEEE.
34. Hammi, B., Zeadally, S., & Khatoun, R. (2019). An empirical investigation of botnet as a service for cyberattacks. *Transactions on Emerging Telecommunications Technologies*, *30*(3), e3537.
35. Rani, D. R., & Geethakumari, G. (2020). A framework for the identification of suspicious packets to detect anti-forensic attacks in the cloud environment. *Peer-to-Peer Networking and Applications*, 1–14.
36. Law, T. K., Lui, J., & Yau, D. K. (2005). You can run, but you can't hide: an effective statistical methodology to trace back DDoS attackers, parallel and distributed systems, *IEEE Transactions on Parallel and Distributed Systems*, *16*(9), 799–813.
37. Yu, S., Tian, Y., Guo, S., & Wu, D. O. (2013). Can we beat DDoS attacks in clouds? *IEEE Transactions on Parallel and Distributed Systems*, *25*(9), 2245–2254.
38. Somani, G., Gaur, M. S., Sanghi, D., Conti, M., & Buyya, R. (2017). Service resizing for quick DDoS mitigation in cloud computing environment. *Annals of Telecommunications*, *72*(5), 237–252.
39. Gilad, Y., Herzberg, A., Sudkovitch, M., & Goberman, M. (2016). CDN-on-demand: An affordable DDoS defense via untrusted clouds. In NDSS.
40. Baciu, G., Wang, Y., & Li, C. (2017). Cognitive visual analytics of multi-dimensional cloud system monitoring data. *International Journal of Software Science and Computational Intelligence (IJSSCI)*, *9*(1), 20–34.
41. Bhushan, K., & Gupta, B. B. (2019). Distributed denial of service (DDoS) attack mitigation in software defined network (SDN)-based cloud computing environment. *Journal of Ambient Intelligence and Humanized Computing*, *10*(5), 1985–1997.
42. Khor, S. H., & Nakao, A. (2011, July). DaaS: DDoS mitigation-as-a-service. In 2011 IEEE/IPSJ International Symposium on Applications and the Internet (pp. 160–171). IEEE.
43. Mathur, M., Madan, M., & Chaudhary, K. (2016). A satiated method for cloud traffic classification in software defined network environment. *International Journal of Cloud Applications and Computing (IJCAC)*, *6*(2), 64–79.
44. Nasiri, A. A., & Derakhshan, F. (2018). Assignment of virtual networks to substrate network for software defined networks. *International Journal of Cloud Applications and Computing (IJCAC)*, *8*(4), 29–48.

45. Tewari, A., & Gupta, B. B. (2020). Security, privacy and trust of different layers in internet-of-things (IoTs) framework. *Future Generation Computer Systems*, *108*, 909–920.

46. Gupta, B. B., & Agrawal, D. P. (Eds.). (2019). *Handbook of research on cloud computing and big data applications in IoT*. IGI Global.

47. Salim, M. M., Rathore, S., & Park, J. H. (2019). Distributed denial of service attacks and its defenses in IoT: A survey. *The Journal of Supercomputing*, 1–44.

48. Tewari, A., & Gupta, B. B. (2017). Cryptanalysis of a novel ultra-lightweight mutual authentication protocol for IoT devices using RFID tags. *The Journal of Supercomputing*, *73*(3), 1085–1102.

49. Zhang, Y., Li, P., & Wang, X. (2019). Intrusion detection for IoT based on improved genetic algorithm and deep belief network. *IEEE Access*, *7*, 31711–31722.

50. Tewari, A., & Gupta, B. B. (2019). A novel ECC-based lightweight authentication protocol for internet of things devices. *International Journal of High Performance Computing and Networking*, *15*(1–2), 106–120.

51. Deshmukh-Bhosale, S., & Sonavane, S. S. (2019). A real-time intrusion detection system for wormhole attack in the RPL based Internet of Things. *Procedia Manufacturing*, *32*, 840–847.

52. Rajagopalan, A., Jagga, M., Kumari, A., & Ali, S. T. (2017, February). A DDoS prevention scheme for session resumption SEA architecture in healthcare IoT. In 2017 3rd International Conference on Computational Intelligence & Communication Technology (CICT) (pp. 1–5). IEEE.

53. Dao, N. N., Phan, T. V., Kim, J., Bauschert, T., & Cho, S. (2017). Securing heterogeneous IoT with intelligent DDoS attack behavior learning. *arXiv preprint arXiv*, 1711.06041.

54. Mehmood, A., Mukherjee, M., Ahmed, S. H., Song, H., & Malik, K. M. (2018). NBC-MAIDS: Naïve Bayesian classification technique in multi-agent system-enriched IDS for securing IoT against DDoS attacks. *The Journal of Supercomputing*, *74*(10), 5156–5170.

55. Dao, N. N., Vu, D. N., Lee, Y., Park, M., & Cho, S. (2018, January). MAEC-X: DDoS prevention leveraging multi-access edge computing. In 2018 International Conference on Information Networking (ICOIN) (pp. 245–248). IEEE.

56. Bhardwaj, K., Miranda, J. C., & Gavrilovska, A. (2018). Towards IoT-DDoS prevention using edge computing. In {USENIX} Workshop on Hot Topics in Edge Computing (HotEdge 18).

57. Sahi, A., Lai, D., Li, Y., & Diykh, M. (2017). An efficient DDoS TCP flood attack detection and prevention system in a cloud environment. *IEEE Access*, *5*, 6036–6048.

58. Doshi, R., Apthorpe, N., & Feamster, N. (2018, May). Machine learning ddos detection for consumer internet of things devices. In 2018 IEEE Security and Privacy Workshops (SPW) (pp. 29–35). IEEE.

59. Kawamura, T., Fukushi, M., Hirano, Y., Fujita, Y., & Hamamoto, Y. (2017, June). An NTP-based detection module for DDoS attacks on IoT. In *2017 IEEE International Conference on Consumer Electronics-Taiwan (ICCE-TW)* (pp. 15–16). IEEE.

60. McDermott, C. D., Majdani, F., & Petrovski, A. V. (2018, July). Botnet detection in the internet of things using deep learning approaches. In 2018 international joint conference on neural networks (IJCNN) (pp. 1–8). IEEE.
61. Mondal, H. S., Hasan, M. T., Hossain, M. B., Rahaman, M. E., & Hasan, R. (2017, December). Enhancing secure cloud computing environment by Detecting DDoS attack using fuzzy logic. In 2017 3rd International Conference on Electrical Information and Communication Technology (EICT) (pp. 1–4). IEEE.
62. Yuan, X., Li, C., & Li, X. (2017, May). DeepDefense: Identifying DDoS attack via deep learning. In 2017 IEEE International Conference on Smart Computing (SMARTCOMP) (pp. 1–8). IEEE.
63. da Silva Cardoso, A. M., Lopes, R. F., Teles, A. S., & Magalhães, F. B. V. (2018, April). Real-time DDoS detection based on complex event processing for IoT. In 2018 *IEEE/ACM Third International Conference on Internet-of-Things Design and Implementation (IoTDI)* (pp. 273–274). IEEE.
64. Anirudh, M., Thileeban, S. A., & Nallathambi, D. J. (2017, January). Use of honeypots for mitigating DoS attacks targeted on IoT networks. In 2017 International conference on computer, communication and signal processing (ICCCSP) (pp. 1–4). IEEE.
65. Yin, D., Zhang, L., & Yang, K. (2018). A DDoS attack detection and mitigation with software-defined Internet of Things framework. *IEEE Access, 6,* 24694–24705.
66. Bhunia, S. S., & Gurusamy, M. (2017, November). Dynamic attack detection and mitigation in IoT using SDN. In 2017 27th International telecommunication networks and applications conference (ITNAC) (pp. 1–6). IEEE.
67. Özçelik, M., Chalabianloo, N., & Gür, G. (2017, August). Software-defined edge defense against IoT-based DDoS. In 2017 IEEE International Conference on Computer and Information Technology (CIT) (pp. 308–313). IEEE.
68. Alharbi, T., Aljuhani, A., & Liu, H. (2017, January). Holistic DDoS mitigation using NFV. In 2017 IEEE 7th Annual Computing and Communication Workshop and Conference (CCWC) (pp. 1–4). IEEE.
69. Liu Y., Dong M., Ota K., Li J., Wu, J. (2018). Deep reinforcement learning based smart mitigation of DDoS flooding in software-defined networks. In 2018 IEEE 23rd International Workshop on Computer Aided Modeling and Design of Communication Links and Networks (CAMAD), Barcelona, Spain, pp. 1–6.

Emerging Solutions for DDoS Attack: Based on SDN and Blockchain Technologies

6

With the manifold advancements in technology, attackers are always one step ahead of defenders. DDoS attack has always been a preferable tool for attackers to incapacitate a target as it is easy to carry out and difficult to detect due to its hierarchical botnet structure. Severity, complexity, and size of DDoS attack always shows an upward trend which calls for new network paradigms to address these constantly changing security threats and requirements. Therefore, this chapter illustrates some new emerging solutions for handling DDoS attacks, i.e., Software-defined Networking (SDN) and blockchain-based solutions. With the latest developments in SDN and its swift and wide-ranging adoption within the network community, several researchers have been actively engaged in the development of SDN-based network security solutions [1]. Blockchain, on the other hand, is the innovative idea of running the public and distributed ledger without any third party's assistance in the untrusted setting. Features of blockchain such as immutability, reliability, cryptography, decentralisation, and verification through digital signatures provide enough reasons to researchers and organisations to invest in this technology for handling cyberattacks.

6.1 SDN AS THE NEW SOLUTION

At present, SDN draws great interest from both academics and business areas. The Open Networking Foundation (ONF) [2] is a non-profit organisation devoted to designing, standardising and promoting SDN. According to the definition of SDN ONF, "In the SDN architecture, the control and data planes are decoupled, network intelligence and state are logically centralised, and the underlying network infrastructure is abstracted from the applications" [3]. As per ONF guidelines, SDN architecture can be divided into three planes namely application layer, control layer and infrastructure layer [4]. These layers are defined in brief in subsequent text.

- Application layer: It largely consists of end-user business applications which consume communications and network services from SDN [4]. It allows end-user applications to communicate with the network devices via controller and also empowers reconfiguration of behaviour or actions of network interface [5]. SDN applications are programmes which can monitor network activity programmatically through the SDN controller [6].
- Control layer: It consists of multiple software-led SDN controllers to provide unified control functionality via open application programming interfaces (APIs) to track network transmission activity through an open interface. The controller has three interfaces to communicate with other SDN planes namely Southbound API, Northbound API, and East/Westbound API [4]. OpenFlow is the de facto standard protocol that regulates the communication between the logically centralised controller and the elements for packet forwarding.
- Data plane: It consists of the resources required to manage an incoming traffic, as well as the resources needed to provide different functionalities, including virtualisation, availability, security, and QoS etc. Data plane consists predominantly of forwarding components, including physical and virtual switches, routers, and access points over an interactive interface that tends to perform packet switching and forwarding.

SDN is intended to be an ideal platform that could significantly contribute to creating effective solutions for detecting and mitigating the DDoS attacks. Figure 6.1 shows the architecture of SDN. The conceptualisation of control and data plane isolation, unprecedented control over infrastructure,

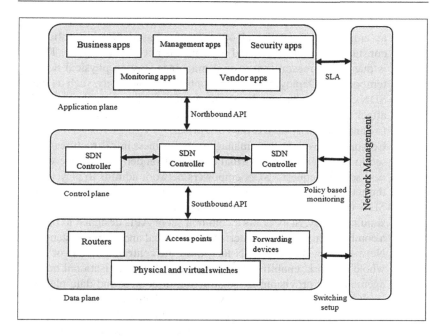

FIGURE 6.1 Architecture of software-defined networking.

and the idea of flow-based traffic make it much easier to track attacks [7]. The research group has attempted to make use of SDN's distinguishing features to improve protection against conventional cyber threats, including DDoS attacks. Although the SDN model offers capabilities to establish appropriate steps to confront DDoS attack, it often carries the vulnerabilities and malfunctions attributable to attacks on controller, for example man in the middle attack, code injection attacks, and DDoS attacks.

6.1.1 Advantages of SDN

There exist several advantages of SDN, for example decoupling of data and control plane, scalability, control over network infrastructure, etc. We will discuss some of the advantages in this section.

- Granular security: A central control point is facilitated by SDN controller for reliable, enterprise-wide dissemination of security and policy information [8]. In other words, it provides centralised security that has drawn attention worldwide. However, virtualisation has rendered network management more difficult, as employing firewall and other content-based filtering policies constantly to monitor virtual machines is not a feasible task. This is due to the reason that virtual machines stay on physical hosts temporarily. Deploying security control onto one body, such as the SDN controller, has the disadvantage of providing a single point of attack, but if applied safely and correctly, SDN will easily be used to handle security across the enterprise.

- Comprehensive enterprise management: Business infrastructure must set up new software and virtual computers on demand to cope with new service requests. SDN empowers network admins to play with the network configuration without adversely affecting the network [9]. SDN controller can monitor physical as well as virtual switches simultaneously. SDN offers a common set of APIs designed to build a combined management interface for physical and virtual systems.

- Network provisioning: SDN facilitates the centralised view of the whole network, enabling the centralisation of organisational management and provisioning. Abstraction of control and data planes leads to increased content delivery rate and enhanced flexibility to provision physical and virtual systems from a central entity [10].

- Lower operational costs: Administrative productivity, efficient resource utilisation at server, better virtualisation functions, and other advantages will contribute to cost savings [11]. While credible proof of savings is still early to demonstrate, SDN minimises total operational costs through administrative savings, as much of the daily network management problems can be streamlined and automated.

- Savings on hardware: SDN has the potential to fully utilise the existing hardware through reconfiguring and reprogramming. Established equipment can be reengineered using SDN controller instructions and less costly equipment can be implemented to better effect as modern systems effectively are "white box" switches with all the intelligence integrated at SDN controller.

- Content delivery: SDN lets the administrator have a view and control over the data flow in the network. The service which lets you control the data flow always allows to control the QoS for different data flows. For example, streaming high-quality content is simpler as SDN increases network sensitivity and responsiveness towards user's seamless experience.

- Abstraction: SDN induces abstraction at every layer in the network. It does the same for cloud computing. It abstracts cloud resources to make it a unified structure. The SDN controller also handles the networking elements that make up large data centre networks.

6.1.2 DDoS Attacks on SDN

SDN guarantees programmability and centralised control that allows a network to be adaptive and effective. Decoupling of data and control plane in SDN provides a promising feature to mitigate DDoS attacks. However, security of SDN is itself a great issue and challenge. We will discuss DDoS attack on every vertical layer of SDN architecture.

6.1.2.1 DDoS attacks on application plane

DDoS attack can be performed in two ways: firstly, on application layer, i.e., on applications which reside on this layer and secondly, on northbound API. Furthermore, SDN cannot resolve the resource or application isolation issue; therefore, one compromised app or exhausted resource can lead to another [12]. In reference [13], authors have proposed a mechanism named FortNOX to handle this attack.

6.1.2.2 DDoS attacks on control plane

SDN controller is embedded with intelligence and thus is responsible for handling network automation, virtualisation, and provisioning. Therefore, SDN controller can act as a single point failure for an organisation and thus is very prone to DDoS attacks [14]. DDoS attack can be performed on all APIs associated with this plane and the SDN controller itself. If organisation has multiple conflicting traffic flow rules, then it might result into DDoS attack on control plane [3]. When data plane communicates with control plane in case of encountering new traffic flow, that means there is no flow rule regarding this new traffic flow in flow table. Data plane handles this situation in two ways: by dropping all data packets or by diverting all new traffic towards control plane. There is no denying in the fact that second option would lead to consumption of high bandwidth at control plane. Possible solutions for these attacks are given in references [15–18].

6.1.2.3 DDoS attacks on data plane

At this layer too, there exist two ways to carry out DDoS attack. The first way is to overwhelm any forwarding device, i.e., switch or router or access point. The second way is to attack southbound API when it is attached to control plane [3]. An attacker can attack any physical device by just sending a header of the data packet. Header of the packet must be stored in the flow table until its entry is returned. Therefore, by sending new data packets with only header information, it can exhaust the memory allocated to flow table at any physical device. Possible solutions for these attacks are given in references [17, 18].

6.1.3 Open Research Issues and Challenges

SDN aims to streamline network operations and provides other numerous benefits [7]. This segment lists the security issues SDN has to encounter while dealing with DDoS attacks.

- Centralisation: SDN brought drastic transformation to the traditional network model by rendering network devices simply as forwarding tools, while the SDN controller is a centralised entity of the whole paradigm. This complete network model introduces simplicity and ease of implementation and updating of network policies, firewalls, routers through a logically centralised entity; however, at the same time SDN controller also serves as single point failure for DDoS attackers. Many researches have been proposed to lessen the effects of centralisation through statistical based, machine-learning-based solutions. Multi-threaded centralised controllers and distributed controllers can be effective solutions while dealing with this issue. However, in references [19, 20], authors have denied the advantages of distributed controllers.
- Scalability: While the decoupling of the control plane and data plane provides certain advantages, it also raises problems of scalability between them. The SDN controller requires a huge amount of computational and processing resources to scale up the network size without affecting performance and response time of the network. In addition, the data plane switches have hardware constraints, for example confined ternary content-addressable memory (TCAM) size results into own network and resource bottlenecks. There are two ways through which this issue can be addressed: first is to employ a distributed SDN controller and second is optimisation of centralised controllers. Proposed mechanisms for the first way are Onix [21], Kandoo [22], and DIFANE [23]. These solutions tend to scale up the data centres in order to enable them to handle millions of flows per second without affecting the responsiveness of the network. Proposed mechanisms for second way are Beacon [24] and NOX-MT [25]. Generally, parallelism has been utilised for optimisation of SDN controller.
- SDN security: Organisations have high security demands when they are providing uninterrupted service to their customers. In

the previous section, we discussed how three layers of SDN architecture are vulnerable not only to DDoS attacks, but also to several other cyberattacks [26]. SDN itself consists of numerous inherited vulnerabilities that are often exploited by attackers to take over the network or to exhaust the resources. Furthermore, hardware constraints of switches and forwarding devices at data layer are also a major security challenge for SDN. Though SDN has reduced the operational and administrative costs for a network to a great extent, however, it still raised many security concerns for researchers. Moreover, centralised nature of SDN controller is also a major issue in this regard.

- Availability of services: Availability of services is the prime feature of any service provider, be it web, cloud computing, or communications. DDoS attack is the major threat to availability, as it tends to exhaust the resources of the victim machine for legitimate users. Unlike distributed nature of traditional network paradigm, SDN is centralised in nature and thus offers single point failure to attackers. If the SDN controller gets DDoS'ed properly, then the whole SDN network gets crippled down, as various software, applications, hardware switches, and forwarding devices are connected to it. Backup or standby controllers [3, 27] can be a solution to this problem. The major disadvantage to this problem is that huge resources are wasted in maintaining and updating this backup controller with the different network states.

- Simulation-based evaluation: The drastic growth in recent DDoS attack incidents show the ineffectiveness of the defensive solutions proposed so far. This is due to the fact that all these solutions have been validated on emulation or simulating tools. Various simulating tools for SDN environment are POX [28], NOX [29], Mininet [30], EstiNet [31] and many more. The major drawback is that the tests are neither precise nor practical relative to those that are performed on the actual hardware in real time. Researchers are still utilising outdated datasets from traditional networks to validate their DDoS defensive mechanisms. These limited tests and small networks are not capable of adequately reflecting the Internet over which hundreds of high-bandwidth DDoS attacks are performed each day. Therefore, considerable efforts to build state-of-the-art and large-scale SDN test beds to verify DDoS identification and mitigation in practical scenarios are needed.

- DDoS traffic and flash crowd events: Unlike the DDoS attack which is a deliberate attempt to undermine the network performance and cause both financial and reputational harm, a flash event leads to a condition where authorised users unexpectedly attempt to send large amounts of access requests. In both cases, QoS and performance of the victim node degrades qualitatively [32]. It is very important that flash events are not misinterpreted as a DDoS attack in order to effectively detect and mitigate the consequences of a DDoS attack. However, the distinction between flash events and DDoS traffic became one of the most complex and challenging facets of network security due to their similar characteristics. Furthermore, unavailability of proper datasets containing both DDoS and flash event traffic has worsened the situation.

- Unavailability of standard datasets: Most widely used datasets are KDD-99 and CAIDA [33] which have become completely obsolete for constantly changing network landscape like SDN. It is likely that if an organisation has become a target of DDoS attacks, it may be hesitant to disclose such databases publicly that theoretically comprise their records of corporate network activity. Therefore, one of the primary factors behind the absence of DDoS attack benchmark datasets may be that these organisations could fear that their credibility might be compromised if they publish such datasets.

- Internet of Things (IoT) and mobile-based botnets: Recent years have seen spikes in development and demand for smart devices. Sophisticated DDoS attackers have pursued advanced techniques to use mobile and IoT botnets to unleash distributed attacks. IoT botnets are capable of generating high-volume disruptions that the Internet has ever witnessed due to its massive availability [34]. On the other hand, mobile botnets consist of smartphones and handheld devices with internet access capabilities that are equally as disastrous as IoT botnets. These threats are impossible to detect by conventional security systems because of their distinguishing characteristics. Mobile botnets are designed to generate long-term results, demand low bandwidth, low battery capacity, and are designed to run in the background in silence [35].

6.2 BLOCKCHAIN AS A SOLUTION TO DDoS ATTACKS

There is no denying the fact that current digital economy is always dependent on the verification by third authoritative party. All digital events have a tendency to rely on some third party to tell us the truth, i.e., it might be some certification authority to tell us how secure a webpage is or to tell us authenticity of a digital signature. Security and privacy provided by the trusted third party is always one thing that all users always look up to [36]. However, one can also not deny the fact that sources and data of these trusted third parties can be manipulated and is prone to several cyberattacks. Here, blockchain technology has the capability to deal with this issue and becomes handy.

6.2.1 Advantages of Blockchain in Mitigating DDoS Attacks

Distributed-consensus-based blockchain technology boost the digital economy where every transaction is verified and validated by participating entities and not by the third party [37]. This technology has proven its capability in security domain also. Following are the advantages of utilising blockchain technology in dealing with DDoS attacks.

- It performs the verification without hampering the privacy of participating users involved and their digital assets.
- The best way blockchain technology can tackle the DDoS attack is by decentralising the whole operation, distributing the code to a vast number of nodes, and making it difficult for the hacker to access the data. Today, DNS effectively maintains a one-to-one unified mapping of IP addresses to domain names (on servers) where access to it is regulated by enabling the people to maintain the domain record about who owns the domain. The same access regulation may be extended to a blockchain, enabling only authorised parties to have respective private keys to update record.
- Another advantage is that blockchain uses encrypted blocks to store data on ledgers. It prevents the third party from making any modifications in the database, rendering it more secure.
- Blockchain has shifted the network model from client–server architecture to decentralisation where there are no specific servers. If there are no specific servers, then there are no specific targets to be attacked by attackers. This can be achieved by using the combined computing capacity and resources of the millions of linked computers in a peer-to-peer (P2P) network protected by a blockchain.
- Blockchain also contains private keys that allow the user to connect with each other.

6.2.2 Architecture of Blockchain

Now, we will discuss general architectural components of a blockchain as companies may modify the structure of a blockchain according to thier requirements [38]. Figure 6.2 shows the structure of a blockchain. The architectural components of a blockchain are transaction, block, P2P network, and consensus algorithm.

- Transaction: A transaction is considered as the primitive building block of a blockchain. A transaction is composed of three entities namely sender address, receiver address, and a value. The owner sends the amount equivalent to value by digitally signing the hash generated by adding the previous transaction and public key of the recipient [39]. This transaction is then broadcasted to the network where the nodes of a network verify all the transaction in the order they appeared. Transactions are bundled in the block and delivered to each node. Every transaction has a time stamp [40].
- Block: Blocks are nothing but the data structures which tend to bundle transactions and then send it to all nodes. Blocks are generated by miner. Mining is the process of creating a valid block that will be accepted by all nodes [41]. It also contains the metadata about transactions.

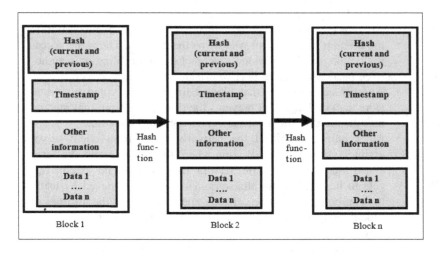

FIGURE 6.2   Blockchain architecture.

- P2P network: A P2P network has an overlay structure which utilises the infrastructure and resources of the underlying network. It has a distributed structure which makes it suitable to be utilised by the blockchain. Blockchain is also a P2P network sitting on the IP protocol [42, 43]. Different nodes contribute equally through consensus algorithm by providing and consuming resources. There is no denying in the fact that decentralisation property of the blockchain is the benefit provided by the P2P network on which it is laid on.
- Consensus algorithm: Consensus algorithm facilitates nodes of a network in keeping their local copy of their blockchain consistent and updated with each other. Consensus algorithm forms the core structure of the blockchain [44, 45]. Proof of Work (PoW), Proof of Stake (PoS), and Simplified Byzantine Fault Tolerance (SBFT) are some of the popular consensus algorithms.

6.2.3 Features of Blockchain

Though bitcoin is the most popular application of blockchain, its applicability in diverse domains is yet to be explored or we can say that it is still in its early phases [46, 47]. Since blockchain allows online transactions to be completed without verification by bank, it also contributes in other applications such as smart contract, Ethereum, and cryptocurrencies [48]. Furthermore, it has also gained immense popularity when merged with other core technologies such as IoT, cloud computing, social media, and many others. Now, in this section we will discuss the reasons behind the immense popularity of blockchain technology.

- Increased capacity: Blockchain has increased the capacity of the network by accommodating large number of users and systems in a decentralised way [49]. Businesses are integrating IoT with blockchain, as blockchain has the immense capacity for such billions of devices.
- Security: There are several mechanisms that ensure the security of a blockchain. Cryptography, hashing functions, and consensus models are some of the factors that provide a strong security to a blockchain ledger [50]. It is difficult for an attacker to tamper the data, as modification made in one block leads to subsequent modification in other blocks too. Furthermore, consensus term refers to ability of the participating nodes of a distributed blockchain network to settle down with the true state of the system coherently,

i.e., validity of the transactions. Consensus models also play a very important role in ensuring security of a blockchain network.

- Immutability: This term refers to the ability of the distributed nodes of a blockchain network to prevent alteration of transactions that have been validated by the nodes through consensus models [51–53]. A centralised database always tends to rely on some third party to provide security to its data. However, blockchain like bitcoin attempts to keep its ledgers in never-ending state of forwarding momentum.
- Decentralisation: It refers to the fact that blockchain does not have any governing authority, i.e., no one will look after the working of a blockchain. Instead, a group of distributed nodes would maintain the online records or digital events through consensus [52]. As there is no governing authority on a blockchain, one could easily access his digital assets from anywhere through the web.
- Faster settlement: Sometimes banks take days to process a transaction. Moreover, bank systems can also be corrupted. Blockchain systems offer quicker settlement services compared to traditional bank systems [54]. Smart contract is an attempt towards faster settlements for any type of contract.
- Minting: Blockchain provides numerous ways to mint problem of manipulation through many ways. It has the great scope in the countries where mining is still the most frequent method [55, 56]. However, blockchain introduces PoW as the approach through which a user can prove his involvement in some considerable computational work.

6.2.4 Open Challenges and Issues in Blockchain Technology

Despite the fact that blockchain has immense potential, it is facing few technical challenges. These technical issues lead to its slow adoption among organisations. Scalability, restricted inter-operability, lack of blockchain developers, standardisation issues, large energy requirements, and the lack of regulatory authority are some of the major issues in this technology. We will discuss these challenges in detail in following section:

- Scalability: Reasons behind immense popularity of blockchain are its distributed nature and transparency across various platforms. A higher number of nodes in a network enhance the benefits yielded by the blockchain. However, one cannot deny the fact that blockchain cannot support the large number of users effectively, i.e., transaction throughput is longer while computation is costlier. Many solutions have been proposed to address scalability issue, namely, lightning networks and sharding. Lightning network is a layer of two protocols. It offers off-chain settlement among participants to enable faster and non-costlier transactions. In sharding, nodes are grouped into smaller networks or shards which are responsible for transaction specific to their shard.

• Interoperability: With almost 2500 cryptocurrencies and numerous distributed ledger technology-based projects, there exist several blockchains in the market. These blockchains work in isolation and does not communicate with other P2P networks. There exist no standardisation measures that may allow seamless integration of these different types of blockchains. From the past few years, researchers have come up with the solutions for interoperability issue, for example, Ark [57]. Ark provides the Smartbridge architecture between two incompatible blockchains and provides a way to communicate. Another solution is Cosmos, which utilises the Inter-communication Blockchain (IBC) protocol to facilitate blockchains to come out from their isolation.

• Limited blockchain developers: It is a matter of fact that advent of new ground-breaking technology takes finite time to be employed by all organisations. Moreover, it took more time for developers to adapt with it. Blockchain is still in its infancy due to which there are only a handful of skilled developers [58]. The lack of skilled developers for managing and operating blockchain technology leads to slow rate of innovations. There is no denying in the fact that there are enough job demands in this field, but the availability of skilled and knowledgeable developers is very low.

• Standardisation: There exist no universal benchmarks or standards for blockchain development or inter-blockchain communication. Good standardisation models help in achieving cost-efficient blockchains and better consensus algorithms. Lack of uniformity across all blockchain platforms results into mass adoption, slow development, unskilled developers, and unsecured blockchains [59, 60]. To deal with this issue, Ethereum launched Ethereum Request for Comments (ERC), which describes the nature or behaviour of an application based on blockchain technology, for example ERC20 has been described for token contracts.

• High energy requirements: PoW was the first consensus algorithm for eradicating the need of centralisation and for verifying the online transactions or events. It requires end users to invest their computational power by solving a mathematical puzzle based on hash functions. Though, it is a distributed consensus algorithm, it also consumes a lot of energy [61]. Experts have predicted that by 2020, bitcoin transaction energy consumption would be as high as consumption of electricity in Denmark city.

So, these are some challenges that blockchain technology is currently facing. Though, it has great potential to be applied to every internet model. However, its complete development is still in its early phases. Now, we will discuss preliminaries of blockchain technology.

6.2.5 Security Issues and Challenges

Though game-theory-based consensus mechanisms and cryptographic puzzles make blockchain technology near unfeasible to hack, these techniques do not claim that security issues for blockchain are non-existent. Inherited security features of blockchain make it resistant to attacks but not immune to them [62, 63]. Table 6.1 lists some security issues and challenges in blockchain technology. In this section, we discuss security issues and challenges of blockchain technology.

- 51% attacks: It is one of the most severe security issues in blockchain. It is an attack in which a group of miners take control of the more than 50% of the network's mining hash rate or computing power. In this attack, attackers prevent new transactions from being confirmed and send them to a halt state. Apart from this, attackers are able to reverse the completed transactions of a block and thus are able to spend coins doubly. In the year 2018, several cryptocurrencies such as ZenCash, Gold, Verge, and Ethereum Classic suffered 51% attacks. Attackers have controlled the huge hash power of bitcoin Gold in such a way after increasing the exchange threshold values by bitcoin Gold, attackers were able to spend coins doubly for many days. Being keen eyed on mining pool, executing mining with a higher hash rate or continuously switching to different consensus algorithm can be viable options to deal with this issue.
- Exchange hacks: Crypto exchange hacks are often nowadays. Crypto exchanges are the most vulnerable targets for the attackers. A crypto exchange is based on centralised single point failure mechanism which makes it more vulnerable to be targeted by attackers. Security problems for exchange hacks can be divided into two categories: client side and server side. In client side category,

TABLE 6.1 Security issues and challenges of blockchain

FEATURE	DESCRIPTION
Scalability	• There has been enormous data quantity in every block of blockchain. • Whenever a new transaction occurs, its complete information has to be added to the ledger. Therefore, as the payment history increases, there exists a danger of sudden failure of blockchain. • Block size is also the main factor for scalability issue. • Response time for getting a transaction validated is usually larger during peak times.
Security management	• Security management in small blockchain-based project is easier to achieve. As the size of the project increases, it is difficult to achieve. • "Who has the right to change the password?" is a debatable point. • Private keys are considered as the digital identity and security credential on blockchain and attackers are always there to steal them. • Complex codes of smart contract can expose open vulnerabilities of the blockchain system.
Standardisation	• Lack of inter-operability between blockchain networks. • Lack of standardisation and benchmarks to regulate blockchain networks. • There is no uniformity in blockchain protocols resulting into inconsistency in blockchain security and mass adoption. • Consistent data communication is needed in open blockchain systems.
Integration in existing infrastructure	• There is a need for restructuring the whole previous hardware and software systems to employ blockchain with their organisation. • Lack of skilled labour in this particular domain for managing complexity of peer-to-peer networks.
Real time	• During peak time, transaction time gets slower. There is a need to enable offline transactions. • Public blockchain systems are inappropriate for real time due to high background activity.
Profitability	• Proof-of-Work consensus mechanism wastes a large amount of resources. However, there exist other consensus mechanisms that provide possible solutions to it. • Transaction costs are also large and central to the systems.

(Continued)

TABLE 6.1   Security issues and challenges of blockchain (*Continued*)

FEATURE	DESCRIPTION
Lack of awareness and understanding	• Main challenge of blockchain technology is that small and medium businesses are unaware of this technology and its functionalities. • There is lack of investment from small and medium businesses.
Productivity paradox	• Speed and efficiency of blockchain in peer-to-peer network comes at the cost of high aggregate cost. • Every node tends to perform the same task as other nodes perform at the same time because every node attempts to mine the other block to find the solution at the earliest.
Security and privacy challenges	• Pseudo anonymity feature of cryptocurrency raises some serious security and privacy issues in blockchain as some applications of blockchain need smart transactions and contract leads to known digital identity. • Though, blockchains are more secure than traditional computer systems, however, attackers can attack the applications built on blockchain.
Environmental cost	• Huge energy consumption of blockchain leads to adverse effects on environment. • Blockchain are built on cryptocurrencies like bitcoin and consensus mechanisms like PoW that consume a large amount of resources for validating the transactions.

there exist many issues like cross site scripting attacks (XSS), open redirects which facilitate attacker in performing phishing-like attack, and issues related to SSL. An XSS attack injects malicious Java script into the web page that successfully extracts the wallet address. Attackers can redirect user to a seemingly legitimate crypto exchange link through open redirects. In this attack, a link with original exchange domain can make a user to download a malicious script unknowingly. In server side category, key-value injections, race conditions, and authentication issues are some of the challenges.

• Social engineering: Social engineering is also one of the major challenges that blockchain technology is currently facing. It comes in many forms but its main motive is always to steal private keys, login credentials, or cryptocurrencies. Phishing is the most common social engineering attack [64]. Some fake mails can be sent by attackers with information like enhancing wallet security through two-factor authentication mechanisms. Users are convinced to send their login credentials through these kinds of mails.

- Software flaws: Though blockchain technology has proved its worth by dealing with all types of attacks, the applications that utilise this technology are still prone to many bugs. In the previous year, the damage associated with software bugs in crypto-wallets and decentralised apps was almost $24 million. It is very important that any software application that is built on top of the Distributed ledger technology (DLT) must undergo rigorous testing and verification. Testing process should include penetration testing, code reviews, and audits for smart contract. Before using any blockchain-based application, one must ensure that that it must undergo through a third-party scrutiny process.

- Malware: It is the most common challenge to the security of any online process. In blockchain technology, it is related to malicious block-mining software, crypto-exchange hack codes, or any other code that can shut down the servers or steal cryptocurrencies from a user, for example, cryptojacking malware. It is the type of malware which exploits vulnerabilities of blockchain and cryptocurrencies. This malware helps attackers to have unauthorised access of a computer's resources to mine cryptocurrencies. This malware does not steal currencies implicitly but induces performance issues like create backdoors for other types of malicious codes. Vigilance of users can help them dodging these types of malware.

6.2.6 Blockchain Vulnerabilities

Blockchain-based cloud is executable only if majority of the nodes in the network are honest and authorised [65]. In the cloud environment, it is possible to have malicious nodes that can attack consensus or mining process of the blockchain. Now, we will study the vulnerabilities present in blockchain cloud.

- Selfish mining attack: In blockchain, it is very difficult task to handle mining process by a single miner as there is huge requirement of computational resources. It is a general practice where multiple miners form a pool to solve hard cryptographic puzzle and share the incentives among the group after mining the block successfully. Blockchain experts believe that a group of selfish miners can intentionally invalidate the computational work of honest miners through selfish mining strategies and easily oppress the incentives of the honest miners in the network [66]. In this attack, a malicious miner from a group of miners who try to withhold a validated block from being disseminated to the rest of the network. While the selfish miner keeps the validated block, rest of the group is busy in mining the next block. Due to this act of keeping validated block, selfish miner can demonstrate more PoW than other miners in the group and can claim financial rewards more than other miners. In other words, a selfish miner tends to maintain its own private chain and discloses it opportunistically to the network to gain more rewards. There can be present more than one selfish miner in the mining pool.

- Double spending attack: This vulnerability is generally associated with bitcoin where adversaries tend to use the same digital cryptocurrency for two transactions or more than one. In general terms, if a user carried out the second transaction with the already used validated data, then it is called double spending attack [67]. It is easy for attackers to regenerate digital currency. A cryptocurrency is nothing but a digital file which can be easily copied. Moreover, there is no central authority to monitor the double spending problem. An attacker is keeping the original copy of digital currency in its wallet while exploiting its copies for multiple transactions. This attack is independent of hash rate employed by the blockchain. This double spending coin problem is not feasible in real life, i.e., with physical currency.

- Eclipse attack: This attack is performed in decentralised environment in which an attacker targets an individual node rather than a whole network by isolating it. It is very similar to the Sybil attack. In this attack, attacker tries to flood the blockchain network with fake peers to make the adversary-controlled nodes as the peers of target node. This attack exploits the P2P architecture of the blockchain environment. This attack obstructs the view of the target node regarding the rest of the network by controlling incoming and outgoing communication of the victim node [68]. First an attacker floods the victim node with the IP addresses of fake peers to which victim likely to react upon after restart of the software. Attacker either waits for the restart or it can be forced through any attack like DDoS attack.

- Block discarding attack: Broadcasting of mined block is very important step in smooth running of a blockchain. This attack is carried out by the attacker with a privilege of good hold of network connections compared to a normal node. An attacker intentionally

inserts slave nodes in the network to enhance its network supe-
riority. The benefit of placing slave nodes in the network is that
attacker could get instant information about freshly mined block
and immediately disseminate the attacker's block ahead of other
blocks to discard them [64]. Apart from block discarding attack,
there is one more attack named as difficulty raising attack in which
hashing power of attacker is utilised to increase the difficulty level
of cryptographic puzzle.

- Block holding attack: In this attack, malicious miner tends to
  reduce the expected revenue of the pool by choosing not to publish any block ever but actually joins to mine the block. It is also
  known as sabotage attack in which attacker makes everyone
  loose [69].

- Anonymity in blockchain-based cloud: Since transactions are per-
  manently stored in blockchain to which everyone in the network
  has access, any user in the network can see the transaction history
  related to any bitcoin address. Privacy of a user will not get compromised unless user discloses it during any transaction or in any
  special situation. Therefore, bitcoin is anonymous to some extent
  as anyone can create bitcoin address but tracing to the real user
  is not a feasible task [70]. Almost anonymous feature of bitcoin
  draws the attention of many attackers as it facilitates the illegal
  transactions in blockchain. To increase the degree of anonymity in blockchain, users are encouraged to have multiple bitcoin
  addresses.

6.3 CHAPTER SUMMARY

As a new network technology, SDN has a bright future with security being
one of the most important and crucial needs. DDoS attacks have progressed
in complexity, and major attacks are conducted with increasing frequency
and scale each year, responsible for attacking large corporations, data centres, and other companies. New-flow-based DDoS attacks have posed major
security issues in SDN by raising various security problems and risks to the
infrastructure, and prompting the need for ongoing research activities to
build new security defences. On the other hand, blockchain is another promising solution for dealing with DDoS attacks. Decentralisation, immutability,
transparency, immunity against cyberattacks are some of the features that
draw attention globally.

REFERENCES

1. Bhushan, K., & Gupta, B. B. (2019). Distributed denial of service (DDoS) attack mitigation in software defined network (SDN)-based cloud computing environment. *Journal of Ambient Intelligence and Humanized Computing*, *10*(5), 1985–1997.
2. Open Networking Foundation. (2020, September). [Online]. Available: https://www.opennetworking.org/
3. Sezer, S., Scott-Hayward, S., Chouhan, P. K., Fraser, B., Lake, D., Finnegan, J., & Rao, N. (2013). Are we ready for SDN? Implementation challenges for software-defined networks. *IEEE Communications Magazine*, *51*(7), 36–43.
4. Jarraya, Y., Madi, T., & Debbabi, M. (2014). A survey and a layered taxonomy of software-defined networking. *IEEE Communications Surveys & Tutorials*, *16*(4), 1955–1980.
5. Nasiri, A. A., & Derakhshan, F. (2018). Assignment of virtual networks to substrate network for software defined networks. *International Journal of Cloud Applications and Computing (IJCAC)*, *8*(4), 29–48.
6. Mathur, M., Madan, M., & Chaudhary, K. (2016). A Satiated Method for Cloud Traffic Classification in Software Defined Network Environment. *International Journal of Cloud Applications and Computing (IJCAC)*, *6*(2), 64–79.
7. Singh, M. P., & Bhandari, A. (2020). New-flow based DDoS attacks in SDN: Taxonomy, rationales, and research challenges. Computer Communications, 154, 509–527.
8. Dahiya, A., & Gupta, B. B. (2019). A PBNM and economic incentive-based defensive mechanism against DDoS attacks. Enterprise Information Systems, 1–21.
9. Izumi, S., Hata, M., Takahira, H., Soylu, M., Edo, A., Abe, T., & Suganuma, T. (2017). A proposal of SDN based disaster-aware smart routing for highly-available information storage systems and its evaluation. *International Journal of Software Science and Computational Intelligence (IJSSCI)*, *9*(1), 69–83.
10. Mishra, A., Gupta, N., & Gupta, B. B. (2020). Security threats and recent countermeasures in cloud computing. In *Modern Principles, Practices, and Algorithms for Cloud Security* (pp. 145–161). IGI Global.
11. Sultana, N., Chilamkurti, N., Peng, W., & Alhadad, R. (2019). Survey on SDN based network intrusion detection system using machine learning approaches. *Peer-to-Peer Networking and Applications*, *12*(2), 493–501.
12. Kreutz, D., Ramos, F. M., & Verissimo, P. (2013, August). Towards secure and dependable software-defined networks. In *Proceedings of the Second ACM SIGCOMM Workshop on Hot Topics in Software Defined networking* (pp. 55–60).
13. P. Porras, S. Shin, V. Yegneswaran, M. Fong, M. Tyson, & G. Gu. (2012). A security enforcement kernel for openflow networks. In *Proceedings of First Workshop on Hot Topics in Software Defined Networks* (pp. 121–126).
14. Myint Oo, M., Kamolphiwong, S., Kamolphiwong, T., & Vasupongayya, S. (2019). Advanced support vector machine-(ASVM-) based detection for distributed denial of service (DDoS) attack on software defined networking (SDN). *Journal of Computer Networks and Communications*.

15. Mousavi, S. M. (2014). *Early detection of DDoS attacks in software defined networks controller* (Doctoral dissertation, Carleton University).
16. Liyanage, M., Ylianttila, M., & Gurtov, A. (2014, June). Securing the control channel of software-defined mobile networks. In *Proceedings of IEEE International Symposium on a World of Wireless, Mobile and Multimedia Networks 2014* (pp. 1–6). IEEE.
17. Shin, S., Yegneswaran, V., Porras, P., & Gu, G. (2013, November). Avantguard: Scalable and vigilant switch flow management in software-defined networks. In *Proceedings of the 2013 ACM SIGSAC conference on Computer & Communications Security* (pp. 413–424).
18. Klöti, R., Kotronis, V., & Smith, P. (2013, October). OpenFlow: A security analysis. In *2013 21st IEEE International Conference on Network Protocols (ICNP)* (pp. 1–6). IEEE.
19. Hamid, S., Bawany, N. Z., & Shamsi, J. A. (2017). ReCSDN: Resilient controller for software defined networks. *International Journal of Advanced Computer Science and Applications, 8*(8), 202–208.
20. Wang, Y., Hu, T., Tang, G., Xie, J., & Lu, J. (2019). SGS: Safe-guard scheme for protecting control plane against DDoS attacks in software-defined networking. *IEEE Access, 7,* 34699–34710.
21. Koponen, T., Casado, M., Gude, N., Stribling J., Poutievski L., Zhu M., Ramanathan R., Iwata J., Inoue H., Hama T., et al. (2010). Onix: A distributed control platform for large-scale production networks. *OSDI, 10,* 1–6.
22. Hassas Yeganeh, S., Ganjali Y. (2012). Kandoo: A framework for efficient and scalable offloading of control applications. In *Proceedings of the First Workshop on Hot Topics in Software Defined Networks, HotSDN '12, Association for Computing Machinery,* New York, NY, USA (pp. 19–24).
23. Yu, M., Rexford, J., Freedman M. J., Wang, J. (2010). Scalable flow-based networking with DIFANE. In *Proceedings of the ACM SIGCOMM 2010 Conference, SIGCOMM '10, Association for Computing Machinery,* New York, NY, USA (pp. 351–362).
24. Erickson. D. (2013). The beacon openflow controller. In *Proceedings of the Second ACM SIGCOMM Workshop on Hot Topics in Software Defined Networking, HotSDN '13, Association for Computing Machinery,* New York, NY, USA (pp. 13–18).
25. Tootoonchian, A., Gorbunov, S., Ganjali, Y., Casado, M., Sherwood, R. (2012). On controller performance in software-defined networks. In 2nd USENIX Workshop on Hot Topics in Management of Internet, Cloud, and Enterprise Networks and Services, Hot-ICE 12, USENIX Association, San Jose, CA.
26. DDoS threat report 2018 Q2, 2018, https://www.nexusguard.com/threatreport-q2-2018
27. Botelho, F., Bessani, A., Ramos, F. M., & Ferreira, P. (2014, September). On the design of practical fault-tolerant SDN controllers. In 2014 third European workshop on software defined networks (pp. 73–78). IEEE.
28. POX controller, https://openflow.stanford.edu/display/ONL/POX+Wiki.html, accessed: July 2020
29. Gude, N., Koponen, T., Pettit, J., Pfaff, B., Casado, M., McKeown, N., & Shenker, S. (2008). NOX: Towards an operating system for networks. *ACM SIGCOMM Computer Communication Review, 38*(3), 105–110.

30. An instant virtual network on your laptop (or other PC), http://mininet.org/, (Accessed July 2020)
31. Wang, S. Y., Chou, C. L., & Yang, C. M. (2013). EstiNet openflow network simulator and emulator. *IEEE Communications Magazine*, *51*(9), 110–117.
32. Bhandari, A., Sangal, A. L., & Kumar, K. (2016). Characterizing flash events and distributed denial-of-service attacks: An empirical investigation. *Security and Communication Networks*, *9*(13), 2222–2239.
33. CAIDA Ddos attack dataset, 2007, https://www.caida.org/data/passive/ddos20070804_dataset.xml, July 2020
34. Oct 2016 DYN/DDoS attack, 2016, http://www.red5security.com/, (Accessed 23 July 2020)
35. Faghani, M. R., & Nguyen, U. T. (2019). Mobile botnets meet social networks: Design and analysis of a new type of botnet. *International Journal of Information Security*, *18*(4), 423–449.
36. Koshy, P., Koshy, D., & McDaniel, P. (2014, March). An analysis of anonymity in bitcoin using p2p network traffic. *In* International Conference on Financial Cryptography and Data Security, Springer, Berlin, Heidelberg (pp. 469–485).
37. Peters, G. W. & Panayi, E. (2015). Understanding modern banking ledgers through blockchain technologies: Future of transaction processing and smart contracts on the internet of money, *Social Science Research Network*.
38. Atzei, N., Bartoletti, M., & Cimoli, T. (2017, April). A survey of attacks on ethereum smart contracts (sok). In International Conference on Principles of Security and Trust, Springer, Berlin, Heidelberg (pp. 164–186).
39. Vasek, M., Thornton, M., & Moore, T. (2014, March). Empirical analysis of denial-of-service attacks in the Bitcoin ecosystem. In International conference on financial cryptography and data security, Springer, Berlin, Heidelberg (pp. 57–71).
40. Niranjanamurthy, M., Nithya, B. N., & Jagannatha, S. (2019). Analysis of blockchain technology: Pros, cons and SWOT. *Cluster Computing*, *22*(6), 14743–14757.
41. Xu, X., Pautasso, C., Zhu, L., Gramoli, V., Ponomarev, A., Tran, A. B., & Chen, S. (2016, April). The blockchain as a software connector. In *2016 13th Working IEEE/IFIP Conference on Software Architecture (WICSA)* (pp. 182–191). IEEE.
42. Wang, X., Zha, X., Ni, W., Liu, R. P., Guo, Y. J., Niu, X., & Zheng, K. (2019). Survey on blockchain for Internet of Things. *Computer Communications*, *136*, 10–29.
43. Feng, Q., He, D., Zeadally, S., Khan, M. K., & Kumar, N. (2019). A survey on privacy protection in blockchain system. *Journal of Network and Computer Applications*, *126*, 45–58.
44. Gueta, G. G., Abraham, I., Grossman, S., Malkhi, D., Pinkas, B., Reiter, M., … & Tomescu, A. (2019, June). SBFT: A scalable and decentralized trust infrastructure. In *2019 49th Annual IEEE/IFIP international conference on dependable systems and networks (DSN)* (pp. 568–580). IEEE.
45. Mingxiao, D., Xiaofeng, M., Zhe, Z., Xiangwei, W., & Qijun, C. (2017, October). A review on consensus algorithm of blockchain. In *2017 IEEE International Conference on Systems, Man, and Cybernetics (SMC)* (pp. 2567–2572). IEEE.

46. Sharples, M. and Domingue, J. (2015). The blockchain and kudos: A distributed system for educational record, reputation and reward. In *Proceedings of 11th European Conference on Technology Enhanced Learning (EC-TEL 2015)*, Lyon, France (pp.490–496).

47. Biryukov, A., Khovratovich, D., & Pustogarov, I. (2014, November). Deanonymisation of clients in Bitcoin P2P network. In *Proceedings of the 2014 ACM SIGSAC Conference on Computer and Communications Security* (pp. 15–29).

48. Tschorsch, F. and Scheuermann, B. (2016). Bitcoin and beyond: a technical survey on decentralized digital currencies. *IEEE Communications Surveys Tutorials*, *18*(3), 2084–2123.

49. Vukoli'c, M. (2015). The quest for scalable blockchain fabric: Proof-of-work vs. BFT replication. In International Workshop on Open Problems in Network Security, Zurich, Switzerland (pp.112–125).

50. Zheng, Z., Xie, S., Dai, H., Chen, X. and Wang, H. (2017). An overview of blockchain technology: Architecture, consensus, and future trends. In *Proceedings of the 2017 IEEE BigData Congress*, Honolulu, Hawaii, USA (pp.557–564).

51. Sompolinsky, Y., & Zohar, A. (2015, January). Secure high-rate transaction processing in bitcoin. In International Conference on Financial Cryptography and Data Security (pp. 507–527). Springer, Berlin, Heidelberg.

52. Luu, L., Narayanan, V., Zheng, C., Baweja, K., Gilbert, S., & Saxena, P. (2016, October). A secure sharding protocol for open blockchains. In *Proceedings of the 2016 ACM SIGSAC Conference on Computer and Communications Security* (pp. 17–30).

53. Karame, G., Androulaki, E., & Capkun, S. (2012). Two bitcoins at the price of one? Double-spending attacks on fast payments in bitcoin. *IACR Cryptol. ePrint Arch.*, 2012(248).

54. Beck, R., Müller-Bloch, C., & King, J. L. (2018). Governance in the blockchain economy: A framework and research agenda. *Journal of the Association for Information Systems*, *19*(10), 1.

55. Sharma, P. K., Moon, S. Y., & Park, J. H. (2017). Block-VN: A distributed blockchain based vehicular network architecture in smart city. *Journal of Information Processing Systems*, *13*(1), 184–195.

56. Leiding, B., Memarmoshrefi, P., & Hogrefe, D. (2016, September). Self-managed and blockchain-based vehicular ad-hoc networks. In *Proceedings of the 2016 ACM International Joint Conference on Pervasive and Ubiquitous Computing: Adjunct* (pp. 137–140).

57. Travis W. What is the ARK SmartBridge, and How Does it Work? Available: https://blog.ark.io/what-is-the-ark-smartbridge-and-how-does-it-work-1dd7fb1e17a0

58. Ouaguid, A., Abghour, N., & Ouzzif, M. (2018). A novel security framework for managing android permissions using blockchain technology. *International Journal of Cloud Applications and Computing (IJCAC)*, *8*(1), 55–79.

59. Sumathi, M., & Sangeetha, S. (2020). Blockchain based sensitive attribute storage and access monitoring in banking system. *International Journal of Cloud Applications and Computing (IJCAC)*, *10*(2), 77–92.

60. Singh, N., & Vardhan, M. (2019). Distributed ledger technology based property transaction system with support for iot devices. *International Journal of Cloud Applications and Computing (IJCAC)*, *9*(2), 60–78.

61. Kosba, A., Miller, A., Shi, E., Wen, Z., & Papamanthou, C. (2016). Hawk: the blockchain model of cryptography and privacy-preserving smart contracts. In *Proceedings of IEEE Symposium on Security and Privacy (SP)*, San Jose, CA, USA (pp. 839–858).

62. Kumar, N. M., & Mallick, P. K. (2018). Blockchain technology for security issues and challenges in IoT. *Procedia Computer Science, 132,* 1815–1823.

63. Joshi, A. P., Han, M., & Wang, Y. (2018). A survey on security and privacy issues of blockchain technology. *Mathematical Foundations of Computing, 1*(2), 121.

64. Bahack, L. (2013). Theoretical bitcoin attacks with less than half of the computational power (draft). *arXiv preprint arXiv, 1312.7013.*

65. Tosh, D. K., Shetty, S., Liang, X., Kamhoua, C. A., Kwiat, K. A., & Njilla, L. (2017, May). Security implications of blockchain cloud with analysis of block withholding attack. In *2017 17th IEEE/ACM International Symposium on Cluster, Cloud and Grid Computing (CCGRID)* (pp. 458–467). IEEE.

66. Kim, S. K., Kim, U. M., & Huh, J. H. (2019). A study on improvement of blockchain application to overcome vulnerability of IoT multiplatform security. *Energies, 12*(3), 402.

67. Rosenfeld, M. (2014). Analysis of hashrate-based double spending. *arXiv preprint arXiv, 1402.*2009.

68. Singh, A. (2006). Eclipse attacks on overlay networks: Threats and defenses. In *IEEE INFOCOM.*

69. Courtois, N. T., & Bahack, L. (2014). On subversive miner strategies and block withholding attack in bitcoin digital currency. *arXiv preprint arXiv, 1402.*1718.

70. Song, G., Kim, S., Hwang, H., & Lee, K. (2019, January). Blockchain-based notarization for social media. In *2019 IEEE International Conference on Consumer Electronics (ICCE)* (pp. 1–2). IEEE.

Index